Decisions? Decisions!

A Practical Guide for
Sign Language Professionals

D0863419

OTHER TITLES BY THE AUTHOR

So You Want To Be An Interpreter?
An Introduction to Sign Language Interpreting
(2nd Edition)
(1996)   ISBN: 0-964-0367-3-8

An Audio Dramatization of
So You Want To Be An Interpreter?
An Introduction to Sign Language Interpreting
(1997)   ISBN: 0-964-0367-5-4

A Hands-On Guided Study For
So You Want To Be An Interpreter?
An Introduction to Sign Language Interpreting
(1998)   ISBN: 0--9640367-6-2

For more information or to purchase a book or tape, contact Sign Enhancers: 1-800-767-4461 (V) or 1-888-283-5097 (TTY), or 1-612-906-1099 (fax).

Decisions? Decisions!

A Practical Guide for
Sign Language Professionals

Janice H. Humphrey

H & H Publishers   Amarillo, Texas

Decisions? Decisions!

A Practical Guide for Sign Language Professionals

Copyright © 1999 by H & H Publishers
Amarillo, Texas, USA

ISBN 9640-367-8-9

H & H Publishers
Amarillo, Texas

In Loving Memory

Bob Alcorn

You made me laugh,
You made me think.

You shared yourself
And taught me invaluable
lessons in the process.

You were a true friend,
And are sorely missed!

1945-1996

Table of Contents

Introduction i

    Authority or Endorsement of Guidelines ii

    Objectives iii

    Acknowledgements iv

<u>Chapter One</u>: Coming to Terms 1

    Key Concepts 2

    Ethics and Professional Practitioners................ 5

    Making Ethical Decisions 6

    Professional Standards..................................... 9

    Meta-Ethical Principles 10

**<u>Chapter Two</u>: Models for Ethical
Decision-Making**......................................17

    The Canadian Psychological Association
    Model 18

    The Stadler Model 21

    Sign Language Interpreting Model 24

    Humphrey/Alcorn Decision-Making Model..... 26

Chapter Three: The Ethics of Professional Competence 37

1.0 Be a Competent Practitioner 37

    1.1 Possess bilingual and bicultural knowledge and skills 40

    1.2 Provide only those services for which you are qualified................. 49

    1.3 Understand the constraints and responsibilities of professional roles 56

    1.4 Continue learning to ensure competent service 60

    1.5 Participate actively in applicable professional associations.............. 62

Chapter Four: The Work Ethic of Sign Language Professionals 63

1.0 Maintain Ethical Vigilance 63

    1.1 Regularly reflect and think critically.. 63

    1.2 Participate in collegial giving and receiving of feedback.................... 64

    1.3 Take personal responsibility 65

2.0 Accept Professional Accountability 68

2.1 Claim or imply only those
professional qualifications actually
possessed................................... 68

2.2 Accountability for information
provided 71

3.0 Present a Professional Image
& Presence 77

3.1 Comply with the norms for
personal appearance..................... 77

3.2 Come to work prepared 80

3.3 Services rendered should reflect
professional standards 83

3.4 Take personal responsibility for
quality of service provision........... 84

4.0 Fees for Professional Services................. 85

4.1 Hold needs of clients primary 85

4.2 Be aware of and sensitive to
professional and cultural norms 87

**Chapter Five: The Ethics of Professional
Relationships...91**

1.0 Establish and Maintain Professional
Boundaries 91

1.1 Limit physical contact 93

1.2 Monitor social interactions........... 98

1.3 Maintain psychological
   separation 102

1.4 Do not manipulate a work situation
   for personal benefit 105

2.0 Guard Client's Personal Dignity and
Right to Self-Determination
/Empowerment 107

2.1 Be aware of personal bias or
   reactions 109

2.2 Maintain confidentiality 112

2.3 Inform clients of special
   conditions 116

2.4 Teachers – Create Safe Learning
   Environments 121

3.0 Assume Responsibility for Consumer
Satisfaction and Quality of Service 124

3.1 Confirm client satisfaction 124

3.2 Remove self if unable to meet
   client needs 128

4.0 Relate Effectively Within the System(s)
Involved 132

4.1 Policies, procedures and Lines
   of Authority 132

4.2 Professional consultations 133

4.3 Record Keeping and Legal
   Liability 137

**Appendix A: Guidelines for Ethical
   Decision-Making**..................................... 139

Appendix B: Case Studies 145

   For Interpreters... 145

   For Teachers... 203

**Appendix C: Sample Codes of Ethics and
   Professional Standards**......................... 225

   Psychiatric Nurses Association of Canada.... 225

   The Society of Translators and Interpreters
   of British Columbia.................................... 228

   American Sign Language Teachers Association230

   Statement of Professional Standards,
   Camosun College.. 237

   American Mental Health Counselors
   Association... 239

   Association of Visual Language Interpreters
   of Canada... 253

   Registry of Interpreters for the Deaf 254

References and Reading List 255

Index 259

INTRODUCTION

I am a teacher and interpreter, practicing in the realm of cross-cultural interactions involving members of Deaf and hearing communities and two languages (American Sign Language and English). In my work I have been challenged with the responsibility of making a wide range of decisions.

Professionals, by the very definition, are individuals in a position of trust, who are called upon by their clientele to judiciously and ethically use the power inherent in their positions. Most professions have a codified set of standards defining appropriate behavior. However, it is mandatory that practitioners take a deeper look at the concept of *professionalism* — including one's role/responsibility, behavioral guidelines, ethical issues and the process of professional decision-making, as well as the consequences of unethical choices and unprofessional behavior.

This text seeks to provide a set of broad principles to guide the conduct of Sign Language professionals so trust can be established between them and their students, clients, consumers, colleagues and employers. It does not provide a series of "rules" which a profession or professional organization has imposed. Rather, the reader will find a set of guidelines to direct practitioners as they make decisions and reflect on professional behavior. This will provide practitioners with opportunities to engage in creative, reflective and evaluative thinking that will help them make sound decisions regarding the professional and ethical challenges they encounter.

Throughout the book, the term **Sign Language Professional** is used to refer to practitioners in the following areas of professional practice:

1. Sign Language interpreters;

2. Teachers of American Sign Language; and

3. Teachers in ASL/English interpreter education programs.

In chapters one and two, I discuss the process of making decisions and the relationship of one's moral center and character to ethical decisions. Chapters three, four and five set forth guidelines to support practitioners as they make a variety of professional decisions. Appendix A provides dozens of case studies for interpreters and teachers to which the guidelines may be applied.

AUTHORITY OR ENDORSEMENT OF GUIDELINES

I must be clear regarding the "authority" of statements made herein. In developing this text, I have consulted with over 100 practicing ASL/English interpreters and teachers in both ASL and interpreter education programs. The manuscript was shared with the boards and ethics or professional studies committees of major national organizations in Canada and the U.S.[1] I received extensive input, questions, suggestions and proposed ethical situations that have been incorporated to the best of my ability throughout the text. While the response of both individuals and organizations has been overwhelmingly supportive, the contents of this text do not represent any official organizational endorsement.

OBJECTIVES

The objectives of this text are to:

a) Clarify the relationship between character, values, ethics and morality related to professional behavior and decision-making;

b) Guide Sign Language practitioners in their professional conduct and in the resolution of ethical and behavioral dilemmas;

c) Create a more transparent decision-making process;

d) Encourage a deeper discussion of ethical issues and professional standards among practitioners working as ASL/English interpreters, interpreter educators and ASL instructors;

---

[1] (1) Association of Visual Language Interpreters of Canada (AVLIC), (2) Registry of Interpreters for the Deaf (RID), (3) American Sign Language Teachers Association (ASLTA), and (4) instructors in the ASL Instructor Certificate Program of British Columbia.

e) Provide students an opportunity to grasp the complexities of professional decision-making and individual responsibility as they prepare for entry into professional fields;

f) Provide specific examples of appropriate and inappropriate, ethical and unethical behavior among Sign Language professionals.

ACKNOWLEDGEMENTS

I must acknowledge the many individuals who have assisted me in the development of this book. It is impossible for me to list every person who has provided ideas, feedback, encouragement and support. These include:

❖ William E. Schultz and the Canadian Guidance and Counselling Association whose work gave primary direction to the development of this text;

❖ Students in the Douglas College Program of Sign Language Interpretation in New Westminster, British Columbia, 1996-1999, who generated many of the case studies and used the manuscript as a text which helped me work out many of the "bugs;"

❖ Participants in various workshops I have taught on ethics and professional decision-making, 1996-1999, who gave me case study ideas and asked questions that made me re-think the content of this text numerous times;

❖ Boards of Directors and committee members of (a) the Association of Visual Language Interpreters of Canada; (b) the Registry of Interpreters for the Deaf; and (c) American Sign Language Teacher's Association. They gave their time to read various versions of the manuscript and provided invaluable feedback;

❖ All of the teachers and interpreters who so freely shared their ideas, comments, and suggestions including: John Aintablian, Marna Arnell, Joni Bice, Tracey Block, Byron Bridges, Sherri Burtnik, Roger Carver, Greg Desrosiers, Kirk Ferguson, Suzie Giroux, Ben Hall, Nigel Howard, Janice "JJ" Jickels, Barry Jenkins, Mike Kemp, Shelly Lawrence, Karen Malcolm, Joe McLaughlin, Marie Magirescu, Nathie Marbury, Cheryl Palmer, Cynthia B. Roy, and Debra Russell;

❖ Editors Ophelia Humphrey and Lynn Babcock without whom this book would never have become a reality.

My heartfelt thanks to each and every one of you.

Jan Humphrey
April, **1999**

NOTE: Quotations set off in boxes are taken from *God's Little Instruction Book*, Volumes I, II and III.

A person's true character is revealed in what s/he does when no one is looking.

Dr. Laura Schlesinger

COMING TO TERMS

eth · ic (µthìk) *n.*

1. A principle of right or good conduct or a body of such principles.

2. A system of moral principles or values.

3. **ethics** *(used with a sing. verb).* The study of the general nature of morals and of specific moral choices.

4. **ethics** *(used with a sing. or pl. verb).* The rules or standards governing the conduct of the members of a profession. (Microsoft® Encarta® 98 Encyclopedia)

Many people in today's world are confused about "right behavior," struggling with what is moral and immoral, right and wrong, good and evil, true and untrue, ethical and unethical (Broadus, 1996). This confusion may partly be due to the fact that morals, values and ethics are intertwined.

KEY CONCEPTS

Morality refers to basic principles of right and wrong as defined by a culture. When a group of people live in a community over an extended period of time, a culture emerges that defines what that group of individuals values, believes in or rejects. This forms the moral foundation of the culture — their definition of right and wrong.

Over time many of the behaviors that are defined as wrong or immoral in a culture become codified into political and/or religious laws — thus the concept of **legality**. Virtually every civilization on earth has a codified mandate forbidding taking the life of another and a definition of the consequences in the event someone breaks that law. Exceptions to the law are also spelled out — self defense or when defending one's country in a state of war, for example.

Ethics refers to the way an individual applies her/his "system of moral standards or values" (Webster, 1996) in relationship with others. One's ethics are identified by looking at the decisions made and actions taken — even when no one is looking. "Ethics concerns the way one lives life as a whole; ethics has to do with character" (Baker, 1996).

Character refers to the kind of person one is — "a package of internal moral elements that causes that person to act in certain ways and to make certain decisions consistently in a morally good way" (Baker, 1996). Character is formed over time through repeated activities — habits, practices. People become what they do — not just the values, beliefs or morality they espouse. Character is clarified and made strong through adversity and it is refined through reflection. "One's character shapes the way one sees, molds the way one feels, gives direction to the way one thinks and all of that becomes her/his natural state" (Baker, 1996).

AN EXAMPLE of the interplay of values, morés and law: North American mainstream culture defines stealing as wrong and immoral. Over time, we have written laws defining theft as illegal. When one steals, is caught, prosecuted and found guilty, there will be negative social and legal consequences. As a part of their personal moral or values system, most North Americans believe stealing is wrong. Thus, personal ethics require that we respect the property of others and refraining from stealing. However, to determine one's ethics we must look at decisions made and actions taken when known to no one other than ourselves. In spite of the values declared, many individuals take something that isn't theirs — a pen from work, a towel from the hotel, excess change inadvertently given by a store clerk. Tax forms may not accurately reflect actual income or exemptions. This is a test of personal ethics. One's personal ethics are influenced by the strength of personal moral beliefs when in conflict with a perceived need, interest or potential for profit. The result may be an incongruence between the values we articulate and the decisions and actions taken.

> **"Reputation is built in a moment;**
> **Character is built in a lifetime."**

ETHICS AND PROFESSIONAL PRACTITIONERS

Those we refer to as "professionals" generally possess knowledge and/or skills that their clients, patients, or students do not have. Further, they are in a position to profit from that disparity of knowledge and/or skills. For this reason, the public holds practitioners to a standard of professionalism and ethical practice.

Various professional bodies have articulated, in codes of ethics and behavioral guidelines, the standards of behavior for practitioners in their respective fields (See Appendix C for several samples). These codes and guidelines clearly define and codify ethical behavior. This fosters a standard so clients/consumers[1] can know what to expect from a professional, "thus eliciting trust from the consumer that we will always act morally in our dealings with them" (Fant, 1990). Violation of ethical standards may subject the professional practitioner to penalties ranging from censure to loss of the right to practice.

---

[1] The term used to refer to individuals served by ASL/English interpreters is currently under discussion. Some prefer to use the term "consumer" while others use the term "client." In this text, the term "client" will be used in order to conform to the standard terminology used by other professional fields.

This is done to ensure that professionals hold the interests of those receiving the service paramount over their personal interest or profit (Humphrey & Alcorn, 1995). Codes of ethics regulate, guide and influence professional relationships, serving as a basis for evaluating a practitioner's conduct in relation to those they serve. They form "imposed, values-based expectations which provide a framework to guide us as we engage in professional relationships, transactions, duties and obligations in our society" (Levy, 1993). Thus, professional practitioners are expected to uphold a level of conduct common to all members of that profession, a standard that might be greater or lesser than their personal ethics.

MAKING ETHICAL DECISIONS

In actual practice, one's personal morality will be the decisive factor when moral or ethical decisions are made in the private sectors of your own mind. When your actions are in harmony with your internal system of values and beliefs, you are able to develop consistent, reflective, and appropriate decisions in both personal and professional matters. Thus, others come to trust and rely on your decisions and actions. Victor Frankl, survivor of the Nazi camps in World War II, discusses this phenomenon in his seminal text, *Man's Search for Meaning*. He states, "Our action must consist not in talk but in right action and in right conduct. Life ultimately means taking the responsibility to find the right answer to its problems and to fulfill the tasks which it constantly sets for each individual" (Frankl, 1946).

Making ethical decisions is not a matter of setting down simplistic rules but of making a commitment to "right action" and accepting the consequences. Strong personal moral and ethical judgment translates into principled professional conduct (McCuen, 1983). This is a particularly important concept when one recognizes that professionals often deal with vulnerable individuals, thus putting themselves in a position where they can exploit information, position and/or material goods.

Levy (1993) points out that "if the person receiving professional service is weaker, more vulnerable, less intelligent, more dependent, less capable of exercising good judgment, or disadvantaged, and the professional's position or role makes it possible to exploit such deficits, the degree of ethical responsibility on the professional escalates proportionately." For example, an ASL teacher is in a position to exploit a student because s/he will determine if the student passes a course, stays in a program or is promoted to the next level of study. As such, students may feel they are "required" to bring gifts to the teacher or to do favors when asked, fearing if they don't do so, the teacher may misuse the power of her/his position.

> Professionals are supposed to be
> trustworthy individuals — expected to know
> how to do their work, to come to the task
> prepared, and to be worthy of the trust
> placed in them by their clients, patients,
> parishioners, or students. Professionals are
> expected to deal with sensitive information
> in a discreet manner and they are expected
> to avoid emotional involvement that might
> work to the detriment of their clientele ... It
> is critical, then, that a professional have an
> internalized moral base and sense of ethics
> (Humphrey & Alcorn, p. 256).

For example, if a professional is working with clients who
are receiving some type of government subsidy, s/he might
be able to re-direct part or all of those funds for personal
use. One's personal sense of right and wrong applied to
ethical standards guards against a professional abusing
her/his position of trust or misusing the power inherent in
that position.

Ethics should not be confused with protocol.
Protocol refers to prescribed behavior, procedures and
courtesies, accepted as proper and correct in certain settings
(Webster's, 1996). Examples include things such as standing
when the Judge enters a courtroom or raising one's hand to
be recognized to speak in classroom interactions.

Nor should ethics be confused with legislated behavior demanded of certain professionals. In fact, legal requirements sometimes conflict with ethical guidelines. An example of this is found in the ethical standard for confidentiality versus the legal requirement to report physical or sexual abuse of a vulnerable individual. In cases where laws are broken or actionable damage is inflicted, the law supersedes professional behavioral standards. Thus in the example above, a professional is legally required to report abuse which is disclosed or discovered while working with a client or student of minor age or vulnerable status regardless of conflict with one's professional code of ethics.

PROFESSIONAL STANDARDS

Professional organizations codify behavioral expectations for their members based on broad ethical-moral guidelines. According to Stromberg (1990), professional associations develop codes of ethical behavior in order to:

1) Educate members of the profession regarding what is appropriate and inappropriate behavior;

2) Foster the development of professional goals and norms;

3) Deter inappropriate, offensive or immoral conduct;

4) Guide discipline of offenders;

5) Provide information to clients, patients, consumers,
    and/or students regarding what is acceptable practice
    by members of the specific profession; and

6) Protect the public from unethical practitioners.

META-ETHICAL PRINCIPLES

Professional codes of ethics are generally based on large,
over-riding principles known as meta-ethical principles,
encompassing an extensive range of behavior, morality,
valued rights, and responsibilities. Specific ethical or
behavioral standards such as confidentiality grow out of
these broad principles. The following are examples of meta-
ethical principles.

EXAMPLES OF META-ETHICAL PRINCIPLES	
a) Do no harm (Non-maleficence)	No one should be hurt or harmed as a result of the decision made by a professional.
b) Do Good (Beneficence)	Decisions made should promote the welfare of all.
c) Autonomy (Empowerment)	Decisions made support empowerment of and self-determination by clients, respecting the rights of all individuals to control their own lives, determine their own conduct and choose their own course of action. This requires that the client involved have the ability to understand relevant information and assess the risks and benefits resulting from different decisions.
d) Justice and equality	The professional should be fair and equal in the treatment of all involved when making decisions.
e) Protection of the weak and vulnerable	A professional minimizes inequities by supporting those who are least able to speak for or protect themselves.
f) Responsible caring	Working with appropriate boundaries to foster healthy relationships, avoiding inappropriate dependence on the professional.
g) Integrity in relationships	Dealing truthfully with clients — speaking the truth, keeping promises, behaving ethically.
h) Informed consent	Decisions made involve the client. The professional is to make certain that clients understand contracts and procedures prior to consenting.

AN EXAMPLE OF COMPETING META-ETHICAL PRINCIPLES FROM THE FIELD OF EDUCATION

Many postsecondary institutions offer scholarships and bursaries to assist individuals with the cost of acquiring their education. When decisions are made regarding the recipient of such awards, ethics come into play.

Ethical Dilemma: Should the head of the student finance office unilaterally make the award *(autonomy)*? Should the decision be made in favor of an applicant with limited social and educational background who has interest in the educational program but who demonstrates limited potential *(do no harm)*? Should the winner be an individual who clearly has the aptitude to succeed in the educational program but who has some other resources at their disposal *(do good)*? Should there be a single set of guidelines determining the award winner and in the event more than one person satisfies those requirements, award the scholarship on the basis of the date of application *(justice/equality)*?

> **Personality has the power to
> open doors, but <u>character</u>
> keeps them open.**

AN EXAMPLE OF COMPETING META-ETHICAL PRINCIPLES FROM THE FIELD OF MEDICINE:

At the present time, a growing number of infertile couples are seeking reproductive assistance by means of fertility drugs. Initial results of these drugs were heralded, but incidences of seven and eight babies in a single birth have resulted in a great deal of public debate. The life of the mother is often threatened, multiple babies are always delivered prematurely — resulting in expensive post-natal care and potential life-long intellectual and physical challenges.

Ethical Dilemma: Do couples have a right to conceive (*autonomy*)? Should medical professionals continue to prescribe fertility drugs (*do good*)? Should professionals refuse to support high risk pregnancies and deliveries to reduce danger to the mother and premature births which result in numerous developmental delays (*do no harm*)?

AN EXAMPLE OF COMPETING META-ETHICAL PRINCIPLES FROM THE FIELD OF SIGN LANGUAGE INTERPRETATION:

When working as an ASL/English interpreter in a medical setting, the medical professional asks about the use of certain street drugs, stressing that the procedure will be fatal if the patient has used street drugs at any time in the preceding six-months. Although the client denies any drug use and signs a waiver to permit the procedure, the interpreter has personal knowledge that the client has used street drugs during the time period stated.

Ethical Dilemma: Does the interpreter take a "hands off" position (*autonomy/empowerment*)? Does the interpreter repeat the information about the consequences of death in the face of drug use (*informed consent*)? Does the interpreter speak privately to the medical personnel (*do no harm*)?

SUMMARY   Professional practitioners — who generally possess knowledge and skills that their clients, patients, or students do not have — are required to subscribe to behavioral standards based on a system of moral values society imposes on individuals in a position of trust. These are referred to as "ethics." Ethics regulate and guide professional relationships and serve as a basis for evaluating professional conduct.

Sign Language practitioners need to study, reflect on and personalize ethical guidelines in order to prepare themselves for the variety of professional decisions they must make day to day. They also need to develop an understanding of the decision-making process. This will help them make appropriate choices in actions and reactions as teachers, interpreters, mentors, and/or consultants.

Several decision-making models are presented in Chapter Two and readers are challenged to develop a personalized approach for making ethical choices. In Chapter Three, we will discuss the ethic of professional competence. Chapter Four focuses on guidelines related to the work ethic of Sign Language professionals. Finally, Chapter Five deals with the ethics of interpersonal relationships between professionals and those they serve.

Readers will find the ethical guidelines upon which this text is based in Appendix A, followed by a plethora of case studies in Appendix B. There are 92 case studies for Sign Language interpreters and 30 case studies for teachers which can serve as the basis for study, personal reflection and as a resource for students and practitioners. In Appendix C, readers will find several examples of professional standards and codes of ethics.

MODELS FOR ETHICAL DECISION-MAKING

As Sign Language professionals, we face moral, ethical and legal dilemmas in the course of our daily work. Choices between clearly ethical options and flagrantly unethical ones pose few difficulties for us — unless one is predisposed to be unethical or is motivated purely from self-interest.

The real challenge comes when there are several options, more than one of which is valid. To further complicate matters, there are times when options may be regarded as ethical by some people and unethical by others. At times meta-ethical principles, codes for professional conduct, and personal values will conflict with one another. Options may support different ethical principles, leading to mutually exclusive choices that cannot be concurrently accommodated. The client involved, the setting and the goals held by various participants will influence the appropriate choice.

Making decisions in these cases is no simple matter. Yet we are expected to make difficult or challenging decisions within seconds while engaged in our work. Because of this complexity, it is important to consider several approaches when making ethical decisions. Eventually, you will need to shape the ideas of various decision-making models into a personalized, integrated model that makes sense to you.

A number of authors have produced models and procedures to support thoughtful, reflective, ethical decision-making. For the sake of brevity, we will discuss three of these models in this chapter:

1. Canadian Psychological Association Model;

2. Stadler Model; and

3. Sign Language Interpreting Model.

THE CANADIAN PSYCHOLOGICAL ASSOCIATION MODEL (CPA)

The Canadian Code of Ethics for Psychologists (1986) suggests four meta-ethical principles to guide decision-making. Psychologists are expected to consider each of these principles when making complex decisions. Unlike some models, CPA ranks the four principles in order of importance to guide practitioners when any of the principles are in conflict. The principles are as follows:

CPA'S META-ETHICAL PRINCIPLES	
a) Respect for the dignity of persons	Decisions are based on actions that support the dignity of individual clients being served — except in instances when there is potential danger to the client or others. This principle speaks against bias or discrimination on the part of the practitioner. Further, clients are to be informed of their options in a clear, accessible manner and given opportunity to give consent or to reject procedures. This principle is given greatest weight.
b) Responsible caring	Professionals are expected to be competent, knowledgeable and skilled in all aspects of their work. In addition, their decisions are expected to promote the welfare of the clients and minimize any possible harm to others, while respecting the dignity of all involved. This principle receives second greatest weighting.
c) Integrity in relationships	Weighted third in priority, this principle requires professionals to be open, honest, and free from bias or compromise within professional relationships. Further, practitioners are to avoid (a) fraud or misrepresentation; (b) withholding critical information from clients, and (c) conflicts of interest.
d) Responsibility to Society	Decisions made should support healthy communities and the good of the larger society. This principle is given lowest weighting when in conflict with the other three principles. Thus, respect for a client's dignity, responsible caring on the part of the professional and integrity in relationships supercede the professional's responsibility to society.

CPA DECISION-MAKING MODEL After setting forth this set of meta-ethical principles with a ranking for each, CPA suggests the following model for resolving ethical questions when principles are in conflict:

1) Identify Issues It is important to review the situation to ensure that all relevant issues have been identified.

2) Identify Multiple Courses of Action This type of expansive thinking is important. It prevents our thinking from narrowing in on one choice of action too quickly.

3) Analyze the Consequences Consider short-term, on-going and long-term risks and benefits of each potential course of action in terms of positive and negative effects on the client, the client's family, colleagues, society, the profession and (where applicable) the employing institution.

4) Choose a Course of Action After careful application of the four meta-ethical principles above, select a course of action.

5) Act and Take Responsibility Regardless of the consequences of the decision made, the practitioner must be accountable. This is the classic "the buck stops here" step.

6) Evaluate Course of Action Effective decision-making requires reflection and evaluation. Otherwise, mistakes would go unnoticed and uncorrected. Likewise, successful decisions would lack recognition and reinforcement.

7) Follow Through Any negative consequences of the course of action selected are corrected as quickly as possible. If ethical issues are not resolved, the steps of the process are repeated.

THE STADLER MODEL

In a series of video cassettes dealing with ethical issues titled Confidentiality: The Professional's Dilemma (1985), Holly Stadler sets out four meta-ethical principles, shares her views on ethical behavior and outlines an ethical decision making model.

Stadler's meta-ethical principles are similar to those proposed by CPA in the previous model, although there is no suggestion of weighting or ranking.

STADLER'S META-ETHICAL PRINCIPLES	
a) Do no harm (non-maleficence)	Choices made and actions taken should not negatively impact the client or others.
b) Do good (beneficence)	Choices made/actions taken should benefit (be good for) the client.
c) Autonomy/ empowerment	Choices made/actions taken should support the client's right to self-determination.
d) Equality	All clients should be treated fairly with equal access to resources and opportunities.

As discussed previously, these principles sometimes conflict with one another, creating true ethical dilemmas.

STADLER DECISION-MAKING MODEL Stadler (1985) proposes a four step decision-making model:

1)   Identify competing meta-ethical principles. Review the situation and apply meta-ethical principles.

2)   Implement critical thinking (moral reasoning) strategies.

   a)   Secure additional pertinent information — This is a critical step. Too often we move toward a decision without knowing enough to act. Find out more about the client, identify standards and clarify your role in particular settings, studying applicable ethical guidelines and examining relevant national or state/provincial laws.

   b)   Examine any special circumstances surrounding the particular situation and individuals involved in this specific event.

   c)   Rank moral principles — this will vary among practitioners, depending on one's personal sense of morality, values and personal/professional ethics.

   d)   Consult with colleagues for additional input prior to going further.

3)   Prepare for Action

    a)   Identify goals or desired outcomes such as
        protecting the client or maintaining
        confidentiality;

    b)   List possible actions, taking care to consider all
        possibilities;

    c)   Evaluate the potential positive or negative impact
        of each action identified. Remember to consider
        the client/student, employer, and related others,
        as well as the larger community;

    d)   Identify any competing values (e.g. independence
        vs. personal safety);

    e)   Select a specific course of action; and

    f)   Test that choice in terms of universal and
        community morés and overall justice.

4)   Take and Evaluate Action

Stadler suggests that when decisions are difficult, a professional should consult with a colleague and/or engage in some activities which might support clear thinking (take a walk, breathe deeply, etc). Once certain, the practitioner should take action based on the decision made. When the actions are completed, the professional practitioner should evaluate the outcomes and the overall process.

> **"The best bridge between hope and despair is often a good night's sleep."**

SIGN LANGUAGE INTERPRETING MODEL

Humphrey and Alcorn (1995) proposed a values base from which Sign Language interpreter codes of ethics have evolved. Below you will find those values statements interfaced with meta-ethical principles.

SIGN LANGUAGE INTERPRETING META –ETHICAL PRINCIPLES	
a) Personal dignity and equality	Decisions made respect the right of all people to be treated fairly and with respect.
b) Privacy/ confidentiality	Decisions respect individual privacy and boundaries.
c) Autonomy and self-determination	Decisions support the right of all individuals to take charge of their personal and business affairs without undue influence.
d) Communication access	Decisions made will respect the right of all individuals to clearly communicate in the language/ mode most comfortable to them.
e) Informed consent	Clients have the right to understand contracts, procedures, costs and potential side effects/results before consenting to them.
f) Self evolution	Professional practitioners will participate in life-long learning and professional development. This will support evolution of professional judgement, skills development and decision-making abilities.

HUMPHREY/ALCORN
DECISION-MAKING MODEL

This model is similar to the Stadler Model and emphasizes the importance of applying critical thinking and decision-making skills to the task of resolving ethical dilemmas. These steps require the professional to:

1) Collect all information and facts possible;

2) Identify goals and relevant meta-ethical principles;

3) Note all possible options (divergent and creative thinking);

4) Identify all potential beneficial or negative results growing out of each option;

5) Review foundational goals or principles (reflective thinking);

6) Identify any emotions that may bias or influence judgment;

7) Consult with colleagues as necessary (reflective and evaluative thinking);

8) Rank options (convergent thinking);

9) Take action; and

10) Review and evaluate action taken.

AN OVERVIEW OF DECISION-MAKING MODELS

Canadian Psychological Association (CPA)	Stadler	Humphrey & Alcorn

1) Identify ethical issues.
 	
2) Develop alternatives.
 	
3) Examine Risks and benefits of each alternative.
 	
4) Apply meta-ethical principles:
 	
  a) Respect for the dignity of persons:
 	
  b) Responsible caring;
 	
  c) Integrity in relationships;
 	
  d) Responsibility to society.
 	
5) Take action.
 	
6) Evaluate action.
 	
7) Correct negative consequences (if any).
	1) Identify competing moral principles:
	
	  a) Non-maleficence;
	
	  b) Beneficence;
	
	  c) Autonomy;
	
	  d) Justice.
	
	2) Implement critical thinking (moral reasoning) strategies;
	
	  a) Secure additional information;
	
	  b) Examine special circumstances;
	
	  c) Rank discoveries;
	
	  d) Consult with colleagues if needed.
	
	3) Prepare for action using a problem solving approach.
	
	4) Take and evaluate action:
	
	  a) Centering and strengthening exercises;
	
	  b) Outline concrete steps;
	
	  c) Act;
	
	  d) Evaluate.
		1) Collect all information and facts possible.
		
		2) Identify goals/meta-ethical principles.
		
		3) Note all possible options (divergent and creative thinking).
		
		4) Identify all possible beneficial or negative results growing out of each option.
		
		5) Review foundational goals or principles (reflective thinking).
		
		6) Identify any emotions that may bias or influence judgement.
		
		7) Consult colleagues as necessary (reflective thinking).
		
		8) Rank Options.
		
		9) Take Action.
		
		10) Review and evaluate results and action taken.

DEVELOPING A PERSONALIZED, INTEGRATED MODEL

The three models summarized above are only three of hundreds in the literature. You may want to search out other models before developing your own personalized, integrated model — one that makes sense to you and that fits your value system and personality. To do this, follow these steps:

1) **Identify Meta-Ethical Principles**   Before you can engage in the decision-making process, you must identify the meta-ethical principles upon which you base your professional practice and decisions. Schulz (1994) restates some meta-ethical principles in a way that may be helpful to you in this process.

2) **Review, Compare and Contrast Models** Create a chart similar to the one on the preceding page in which you can compare and contrast the major steps and/or principles that you feel hold greatest value in each model. Next, identify those steps and principles that you feel will be most useful to you. For example, in the three models above, the first step of all three models is very similar and may seem to be a logical first step for you. That may become "step one" in your model.

SCHULTZ'S META-ETHICAL PRINCIPLES	
a) Sanctity of life	Decisions do not put anyone's life in danger, respecting the value and sanctity of all living beings.
b) Not willfully harming others	Choices made and actions taken should not negatively impact the client or others.
c) Keeping Promises	Promises made to clients are taken seriously and are not to be broken.
b) Responsible caring	Professional decisions support healthy, boundary-appropriate caring and relationships, keeping the dignity of others intact.
c) Responsibility to society	Decisions made will support the good of the larger society.
d) Respecting the right for self-determination	All individuals have a right to take charge of their personal and business affairs without undue influence from a third party or the forceful imposition of another's value system. Practitioners will respect this right when making professional decisions.

Remember, in the end the thing that counts is that we did not satisfy ourselves with talking about right choices or debating possible actions (Frankl, 1946; Baker, 1996). Rather, we must take responsibility to find and act on the best answers to the dilemmas we encounter. A commitment to "right action" and accepting the consequences is only possible when an individual has identified the moral principles that form the foundation for professional decisions.

> ## "A minute of thought is worth more than an hour of talk."

3) <u>**Apply Critical Thinking Principles**</u> This step is based on logic, prioritizing meta-ethical principles and beginning the action process (Schultz, 1994). This is done by:

    a)   Generating a list of alternatives considering the risks and benefits of each;

b) Securing additional information and/or consulting with colleagues; and

c) Examining the probable outcomes of various courses of action.

4) **Apply Emotive Techniques**   It is important to balance rational reasoning of steps two and three with emotional thinking. Schultz (1994) suggests that because the process to this point has been fairly cognitive, professionals should now apply emotive techniques. Although there are many strategies you may consider, Schultz suggests the following:

a) Reflect — Take a solitary walk in the woods or park, allowing your emotions to interact with the ethical dilemma being faced;

b) Incubate — Don't rush. Take some time to "sleep on it:" and/or

c) Project the ethical situation into the future — think about the various potential outcomes and scenarios.

5) **Make a Decision, Take Action, Evaluate and Accept Responsibility** Develop and implement a concrete action plan, evaluate the plan and be prepared to correct any negative

consequences that might result from the action taken.

AN EXAMPLE OF THE PROCESS Schulz (1994)

shares a brief example to show how the steps of such a personalized, integrated model might work in actual practice. In this example, Schultz poses that a high school counselor has seen a seventeen-year-old, grade eleven student on numerous occasions. Initially, these visits come as a result of teacher referrals. Teachers find John a "nuisance in the classroom." Over the months, a good relationship develops between the counselor and John, and John frequently just drops by to chat. On one such occasion, John talks about his part-time job at a hardware store and how he makes quite a bit of extra money "lifting" the occasional article from the store and selling it. When the counselor gets more of the details, he is convinced that considerable theft is involved. He doesn't know what to do, since he had promised confidentiality.

WHAT ARE THE KEY ETHICAL ISSUES IN THIS SITUATION?   Confidentiality vs. Legal

Responsibility The counselor has promised confidentiality, yet John's actions are illegal. In the long run, the thefts will probably be discovered and John will be in serious trouble.

APPLICABLE META-ETHICAL PRINCIPLES   Of the six principles identified, Schulz suggests the following principles apply in this situation:

- Keeping promises;

- Responsible caring;

- Not willfully harming others;

- Responsibility to society; and

- Respecting people's rights to control their own destiny.

The counselor considers each of the principles above and what might happen ...

- If he reports the theft;

- If he keeps quiet and continues to work with John; and

- How he can best help John.

Without identifying John, the counselor discusses the situation with another professional, and is advised to "cover yourself — tell the principal."

PRIORITY OF APPLICABLE PRINCIPLES   At this point, the counselor makes a decision. He decides that "responsible caring" and "responsibility to society" carry the greatest priority in this situation.

RISKS TO CONSIDER   The counselor identifies several significant potential outcomes:

- The welfare of society will be supported if the thefts stopped;

- John is at risk if he continues to break the law;

- The relationship between the counselor and his client is threatened if the counselor violates confidentiality;

- If no action is taken, it might be perceived that the counselor condones John's behavior or that the counselor so disregards John that his welfare is insignificant.

SUPERSEDING VALUES   In the face of so many conflicting principles, the counselor asks himself a fourth question: "Will I feel the same way about this situation if I wait a day or two before deciding?"   He decides to "sleep on it" and spends the next 12-hours pondering the question: "How can I best help John and at the same time stop any future theft?"

PROVISIONS AND PRECAUTIONS   The next morning, the counselor makes an appointment with John to inform him that he will have to break confidentiality, since he feels that he will not be acting responsibly if he allows the stealing to continue. He tries to convince John that in the long run he might actually be helping him as well. John is given several options by the counselor regarding the reporting of the theft:

a) John can report the theft to his boss or the police;

b) The counselor can report the theft to John's boss or the police; or

c) John and the counselor can see the appropriate authorities together.

EVALUATION   Decisions and actions taken are best evaluated after a period of time. The immediate results do not always indicate the quality of the decision made.

In this case, John chose to report the theft to the owner of the store and to offer restitution. The store owner agreed to let John make restitution and did not inform the police. However within six months, John was involved in theft again and was arrested by the police.

In evaluating his decision, the counselor felt he had made a good choice since it:

a) Empowered John to make the decision of reporting the theft;

b) Reduced harm to the public by stopping the theft; and

c) Resulted in good — repayment for items stolen and a second chance for John to make choices regarding taking the property of others.

We have provided a variety of case studies in Appendix B to help you practice decision-making skills. In addition, the following chapters outline a variety of ethical guidelines to direct your thinking. Working through these chapters and case studies will help sharpen your own analytical skills and give you practice in making ethical and professional decisions.

THE ETHICS OF
PROFESSIONAL COMPETENCE

1.0   Be A Competent Practitioner

Every profession requires that practitioners in their field be competent to practice. For lawyers, this means knowing the law and being able to properly present a case before the bar. For doctors, this means being familiar with medical conditions and their treatment. For Sign Language practitioners, this includes working as community-endorsed practitioners who are active members of the Deaf community and in affiliated professional associations. Before working as a teacher or interpreter, a competent practitioner has the specific skills, knowledge and ability required to teach or to interpret. This includes knowledge of the subject being taught or interpreted, specialized educational preparation and demonstrated skills (certification).

A competent Sign Language interpreter can be described as having:

a)   Bilingual/bicultural knowledge and skills necessary to determine the intent and spirit of a speaker and to express that intent and spirit in an equivalent manner in the target language and culture;

1.0   Be A Competent Practitioner

b) Flexible communication abilities in order to meet each
    client's preferred language or communication mode and
    to manage register, geographic, gender and age
    variations;

c) Knowledge of setting-specific protocol, the ability to
    behave professionally and to provide competent service,
    given the specific assignment (client, setting, topic of
    interaction, type of skills required, etc);

d) Graduated from appropriate educational programs and
    holding professional certification(s);

e) Demonstrated commitment to continuing professional
    development in order to expand areas of competence
    and better serve clientele.

A competent teacher of Sign Language or ASL/English
interpretation is one who:

a) Has graduated from appropriate educational
    programs, demonstrating mastery of essential
    knowledge in content area;

1.0   Be A Competent Practitioner

b) Holds professional certification(s) demonstrating skill in the evaluation of student performance and the facilitation of learning;

c) Is able to adjust communication and instruction to complement a variety of learning styles and cultural frames of reference;

d) Understands academic systems and protocol, demonstrating ethical and professional behavior in cross-cultural, multilingual settings;

e) Is committed to continuing professional development in order to expand areas of competence and better serve students.

Part of being competent is knowing what one is not qualified to do. One of the most honorable and professional actions a practitioner can take is to decline a job s/he is not able to do well (Humphrey & Alcorn, 1995).

1.0   Be A Competent Practitioner

1.1 Possess bilingual and bicultural knowledge and skills that support appropriate community interaction leading to formal or informal community endorsement.

Sign Language professionals are unique because they work primarily in cross-cultural and multilingual environments. In other words, they work to facilitate communication between the mainstream (hearing) community that uses the majority spoken language and members of a minority (Deaf) community using a visual-gestural language to communicate. This results in some unique elements when defining professional competence in this field.

Bilingual knowledge and skills refers to competence, fluency and flexibility in the use of American Sign Language (ASL) and spoken/written English. It includes the ability to manipulate both languages in order to use them in a variety of registers and settings, including word/sign humor and English-based signs used by some individuals who are Deaf or hard-of-hearing. It also means one can adapt her/his spoken and signed communication in order to:

1.0 Be A Competent Practitioner

a) Accommodate age, gender, geographic and register variations;

b) Communicate effectively with native users of the language as well as with individuals of limited language competence;

c) Use technical, specialized, and general terminology.

In addition, all Sign Language professionals should understand the following aspects of both mainstream hearing and Deaf culture as defined by Philip (1986a, 1986b):

a) *Tangible* (material) — physical items and artifacts representative of a culture such as video-telephones, TTYs, e-mail, visual and auditory alert devices, etc;

b) *Normative* — the values, beliefs and norms of social interaction that can be observed, copied, and eventually learned by a newcomer to the culture including turn-taking signals, greeting and leave-taking behaviors; and

c) *Cognitive* — the unwritten, subtle and complex essence of a culture that is virtually invisible to the foreign sojourner. Conferred community membership determining in-group and out-group status is one example of this aspect of culture.

1.0   Be A Competent Practitioner

Approval as a culturally appropriate, community-endorsed practitioner may be unique to Sign Language professionals, yet it is critical if one is to be accepted by the Deaf community as competent to practice. Although mainstream institutions focus primarily on educational credentials, publications and research when hiring teachers, consultants and others, cultural norms in the Deaf community require that Sign Language professionals subscribe to a different standard.

This is particularly true of ASL teachers. Deaf cultural norms in most communities include the requirement that one who teaches ASL must:

a)   Be both auditorially and culturally Deaf;[1]

b)   Be active in the local Deaf community;

c)   Have resided in the area long enough to be familiar with geographic uniqueness in language and cultural norms; and

d)   Have a formal or informal "stamp of approval" from the Deaf community.[2]

---

[1] This standard varies from community to community. The American Sign Language Teachers Association (ASLTA) holds that the focus should be that teachers are qualified and competent regardless of hearing status. ASLTA certification is one way of insuring that a teacher is qualified to teach ASL whether the individual is deaf or hearing.
[2] Personal communication with Carver, McLaughlin, Kemp, Chan, Magirescu, Jenkins, and Jickels, 1997.

1.0   Be A Competent Practitioner

In some cases, non-deaf individuals are given Deaf community approval to teach ASL. This is rare and is dependent on the availability of Deaf teachers in the geographical area, as well as the linguistic skills, cultural knowledge and attitude of the non-deaf individual.

Similar requirements are held for instructors in interpreting programs and for ASL/English interpreters working in the community, particularly in mental health, medical and legal settings. These individuals are generally required to:

a) Demonstrate bilingual and bicultural knowledge and skills;

b) Be appropriately active in the local Deaf community;

c) Hold appropriate educational credentials and professional certification(s);

d) Reside in the area long enough to be familiar with regional variations in language and cultural norms; and

e) Have formal or informal acceptance to practice from the Deaf community.[3]

---

[3] Ibid.

1.0   Be A Competent Practitioner

Appropriate community interaction: There are certain roles and responsibilities expected of various members of the community. Certain interactions are appropriate only for Deaf community members, while others are open for wider participation. Further, certain community responsibilities exist due to the reciprocity pool in which everyone shares her/his talents and abilities with the larger community (Philip, 1986a, 1986b). For example, hearing individuals are often called upon to share expertise in writing letters, interpreting or explaining phenomena of the mainstream society. College educated Deaf individuals are expected to represent the community in formal settings, such as testifying before governmental hearings or supporting community members who are unable to express themselves in a clear or articulate manner.

Interpreters are expected to interact socially but they are also expected to know how to establish invisible boundaries between themselves and members of the community with whom they work in sensitive settings.

ASL instructor and interpreter educators are expected to demonstrate commitment to the Deaf community by regular, ongoing involvement and by using discretion regarding what they teach their students.

1.0   Be A Competent Practitioner

Interpreters mediate communication between members of the Deaf and the hearing communities. The U.S. Foreign Service Language Index notes that one is not able to interpret between any two languages until s/he is able to manage the languages being used at a level eight out of ten. Thus an interpreter's language abilities must be above average in both English and ASL. Language competency for interpreters also includes the concept of "word attack" skills that help a language user determine the meaning of unfamiliar linguistic items when used in context.

Interpreters are also expected to have a general knowledge of historic and current events in both the Deaf and mainstream communities in order to deal with references that may occur in the utterances being interpreted. They are expected to mediate cultural differences within communication exchanges, thus knowledge of both cultures is imperative. Interpreters need the linguistic, cultural, and social skills that will allow them to interact socially in the Deaf community while protecting any professional relationships with individuals also in attendance at social events.

1.0   Be A Competent Practitioner

APPLYING THE STANDARDS

Fantasie, a sign language interpreter, is getting ready to go to the Friday night gathering of the Deaf community. She has had a busy week! In the last few days she has interpreted:

1. A therapy session — Minnie and Mickey are having some trouble in their relationship.

2. A medical appointment for Brutus who is HIV positive.

3. An emotional meeting between Cinnamon and her employer during which Cinnamon received a strong reprimand and warnings of possible dismissal if certain behaviors don't change.

Upon entering the social gathering, Fantasie notices that there are about 50 people at the party. Remembering that this is a visually based community of people, Fantasie monitors her own facial response to the Deaf individuals she encounters. She spies Minnie, Mickey, Brutus and Cinnamon among those in attendance. Brief eye contact with Cinnamon is met with Cinnamon diverting her eyes and making no indication that she recognizes Fantasie. Brutus comes up to Fantasie and gives her the common greeting hug and engages in conversation about the upcoming Deaf bowling tournament. Mickey and Minnie make eye contact, smile and wave but make no effort to engage Fantasie in conversation. Fantasie reciprocates in kind.

REFLECTING ON FANTASIE'S SITUATION: Fantasie is demonstrating the ability to maintain Deaf community involvement while protecting the identity and any related information learned in interpreted contexts. She has learned to take her cues from each Deaf individual she encounters. If they do not take the initiative to approach or greet her, Fantasie follows suit. When they do engage in some type of social greeting and/or banter, Fantasie reciprocates, steering clear of any dialogue in which topics similar to those that arose in the interpreted event might have been discussed.

1.0   Be A Competent Practitioner

Instructors in interpreting programs should be able to model a variety of interpreting skills for students. This means they must possess bilingual skills equal to those of an interpreter. They are also required to interact socially within the Deaf community. In addition, educational programs should have Deaf community representation in the program and/or on its advisory board.

While ASL instructors are employed to teach Sign Language, there is a level of English competence required in order to read teacher's manuals, complete institutional forms, and to prepare class handouts, exams, etc. However, if one is employed to teach ASL, it is critical that s/he be:

a)   Fluent in ASL;

b)   Familiar with Deaf culture and its rules;

c)   Able to distinguish between ASL and English-based signs; and

d)   Knowledgeable of the structure and linguistic rules of the language.

1.0   Be A Competent Practitioner

APPLYING THE STANDARDS

Beammette is Deaf. She grew up with no Deaf community contact, using speech and speech reading as her primary mode of communication. She first started to sign after going to Gallaudet University at age 16. Now, at age 24, she has a large vocabulary of signs but does not structure her signs according to the grammatical rules of ASL. In addition, she finds it virtually impossible to sign without speaking the sign gloss. Since her return from Gallaudet two years ago, Beammette has been active in the local Deaf club and currently serves as the treasurer.

The local college is now seeking an ASL instructor and Beammette wants to apply. She has a BA degree from Gallaudet in elementary education and has taken one introductory course in ASL linguistics.

However, she learned that Branch is applying for the job. Branch is also Deaf, has been active in the Deaf community since graduating from the residential school for the Deaf where he developed native-like fluency in ASL. Branch has completed three of five courses required to become a certified ASL instructor and is an active member of ALSTA.

Beammette discusses her decision with several members of the Deaf community after which she decides she is not yet ready to teach ASL. She believes she needs greater ASL fluency and more time to learn the social and cultural norms of the Deaf community.

REFLECTING ON BEAMMETTE'S SITUATION:

Beammette is wise to wait before teaching an ASL course. While the local Deaf community is beginning to embrace her, she has not had adequate exposure to ASL or Deaf culture to meet the criteria for informed community endorsement. Further, deferring to Branch demonstrates cultural sensitivity and will earn Beammette "brownie points" within the community.

1.0   Be A Competent Practitioner

1.2   Provide only those services for which you are qualified by training, experience and certification and which are culturally appropriate for you to provide.

Professionals do not deliver services unless they are qualified to do so. When people practice without appropriate education and credentials, the number of horror stories escalates. Clients/students are placed at risk because the quality of service is substandard (Seymour, 1990).

ASL TEACHERS

EDUCATION   Because teachers work in academic settings, it is important for them to hold at least a Bachelor's degree in their field or a closely related field. Individuals teaching ASL must complete training in teaching second languages to adults, developing and interfacing instructional objectives, learning activities, and evaluation.

COMMUNITY ENDORSEMENT Deaf community standards for instructors need to be identified and adhered to by individuals, as well as educational institutions in

1.0   Be A Competent Practitioner

order to have the full support of the Deaf community when offering Sign Language courses. This is sometimes challenging because the definition of "qualified" is sometimes different between the Deaf and the academic communities. Colleges see hearing individuals as "qualified" because they may hold the academic credentials that have been inacessible to members of the Deaf community. The Deaf community measures "qualifications" based on an individual's language abilities and cultural sensitivity. In some areas, the Deaf community has deemed it inappropriate for a non-Deaf individual to teach American Sign Language. In other areas, the Deaf community is comfortable with hearing individuals who satisfy their criteria of "qualified" to teach ASL. Where this is an issue, one solution is to arrange for a team of teachers — one Deaf and one non-Deaf — in order to satisfy both academic and Deaf community requirements.

CERTIFICATION   Certification is a form of professional accreditation or recognition of an individual. It is not enough to have university degrees; most professions expect practitioners to obtain and maintain professional certification(s). For ASL instructors, this would include the Sign Language Instructors of Canada (SLIC) certification or the American Sign Language Teachers Association (ASLTA) certification.

1.0   Be A Competent Practitioner

INTERPRETER EDUCATORS

EDUCATION In the area of Sign Language interpreter education, the Conference of Interpreter Training (CIT) recommends a minimum of a Master's degree with preference for Doctoral degrees.

CERTIFICATION Faculty members in interpreter education programs should hold appropriate professional certifications. For ASL instructors, this would include ASLTA or SLIC documentation. Both Deaf and hearing instructors teaching interpreting courses should hold interpreter certification from AVLIC or RID. Further, faculty members should work to meet the accreditation standards put in place by the Conference of Interpreter Trainers. Knowing these educational standards and failing to satisfy them is inherently unethical.

COMMUNITY ENDORSEMENT   Staff and faculty members of an interpreter education program are expected to satisfy the standards of Deaf community endorsement Among other criteria, there are certain social and community expectations placed on the faculty and staff. By gaining informal community endorsement, the educational

1.0   Be A Competent Practitioner

program has credibility and graduates are embraced by the Deaf community upon graduation.

SIGN LANGUAGE INTERPRETERS

EDUCATION   One can work as an interpreter without a college education, however it is strongly recommended that interpreters strive for at least a Bachelor's degree. This is because of the nature of the work interpreters perform. They need above average language skills and a wide range of world knowledge in order to comprehend and convey the messages being communicated in English and ASL. This requires quick mental processing skills. Advanced education supports an appropriate base and helps develop language processing and critical thinking skills.

CERTIFICATION ASL/English interpreters should work as certified practitioners, holding certification from the Registry of Interpreters for the Deaf (RID) or the Association of Visual Language Interpreters of Canada (AVLIC). While there are some "stepping stones" that can lead a practitioner from entry-level skills to certification such as state/provincial

1.0   Be A Competent Practitioner

screening tools and quality assurance examinations, the goal is to become nationally certified as quickly as possible.

> **"Choice, not chance, determines human destiny."**

PERSONAL ACCOUNTABILITY   The field of interpretation is broad, requiring diverse knowledge and skills. It is critical for an interpreter to recognize the settings, topics and clients for whom s/he is _unable_ to provide top quality service. In these instances, professional ethics require the interpreter to turn down or withdraw from the situation and (where possible) to recommend a qualified professional to do the job. A choice of this type has nothing to do with years of experience, ability or certification. This may happen to both certified and uncertified, experienced and novice interpreters. It is not possible for individuals to be able to do everything. Further there is no negative label attached to the interpreter who turns down or excuses her/himself from working with settings, topics or clients for whom s/he is unable to provide work that measures up to professional standards.

1.0   Be A Competent Practitioner

APPLYING THE STANDARDS

Charlemagne is deaf, attended the residential school for the deaf as a child and married a hearing woman who does not sign. He socializes with members of the hearing community and has had no contact with the Deaf community in his town for over 20 years.

After being laid off from his printing job of 25 years, Charlemagne decided to apply for a job teaching Sign Language at the local college. During an interview for the job, Charlemagne informed the interview committee that he was fluent in ASL and was an active member of the Deaf community. He explained that he was certified to teach — although he didn't mention that he was certified to teach scuba diving, not ASL.

The committee offered Charlemagne the job and he accepted. Once he received the course syllabus and textbook, he realized he was not familiar with much of the terminology and with the approach to instruction. Rather than seek help or clarification, he simply put the materials aside and made up his own lessons, teaching what he thought would be most helpful to the students in the class.

REFLECTING ON CHARLEMAGNE'S SITUATION: Charlemagne ignored every aspect of this ethical guideline. Even though he is audiologically unable to hear, he has not maintained his Deaf community ties and has not used ASL as a regular form of communication. Charlemagne misrepresented his credentials and opted not to follow the established curriculum.

A more appropriate response from Charlemagne would be for him to:

1. Re-establish Deaf community ties and begin to attend some community events;
2. Contact some Deaf acquaintances who are teaching ASL courses and ask if he can observe their classes;
3. Sign up for and take courses or workshops on recent research into ASL, second language instructional methodology, and teaching adults;
4. Join the professional organization of ASL instructors and begin to seek their certification.

1.0   Be A Competent Practitioner

APPLYING THE STANDARDS

Dragonfly has been working professionally as an interpreter for 12 years. She has worked in various secondary and post-secondary educational settings, as well as doing some community interpreting, earning $15 - $20 per hour. Work has been steady and Dragonfly has been able to "hold her head above water" financially. However, her car is in need of major repairs and she needs a new roof on her house. She is not sure where she will find the money for these unplanned expenses.

Yesterday she was contacted by a local hospital asking to place her name on their roster of on-call interpreters. They explained that she would be assigned certain dates for which she must remain available for any medical interpreting needs arising between 6 p.m. and 8 a. m. on week days and 24 hours per day on weekends. In exchange for being on the on-call list, the hospital would pay Dragonfly a monthly retainer of $250 plus $45 per hour for any interpreting she was required to provide (2-hour minimum).

Dragonfly surmised that any calls she received would be primarily of an emergency nature and when asked, the hospital confirmed that. They also noted that the calls would cover everything from pediatric emergencies to psychiatric emergencies. Dragonfly quickly thought over her interpreting experience, education and training. She recognized that she is squeamish around blood and becomes physically sick when confronted with the smell of vomit. She is also aware of the fact that psychiatric settings demand a level of skill and training that she does not possess at this time. As much as she needs the income, she informed the hospital that she would not be able to allow her name to be added to the on-call list at this time.

REFLECTING ON DRAGONFLY'S SITUATION: This scenario presents us with the type of ethical dilemmas many Sign Language professionals encounter — the balance between one's own needs (funds to support one's self and family) and one's responsibility to ensure their clients have the best possible service. Dragonfly made the ethical choice — holding the interests of her clients above her own personal needs. This is difficult to do, especially when the client or agency applies pressure — "But if you don't do it nobody will," "you are better than you think, just give it a try," "anybody is better than nobody." The professional thing to do is to fall back on your own knowledge of yourself and right and wrong as reflected in professional ethics.

1.0   Be A Competent Practitioner

1.3 Understand the constraints and responsibilities of professional roles from both mainstream (hearing) and minority (Deaf) cultural views.

The definition of "professional" varies from culture to culture. In addition, the role and responsibilities of a professional vary accordingly. In the mainstream hearing society of North America, the generally accepted definition of a "professional" is one qualified to provide service based on completion of specialized education, acquisition of professional certification or license, and experience. Further, a professional in the mainstream society is expected to establish an emotional and psychological boundary known as "professional distance." This is the boundary that dictates an "involved but separate" relationship between the practitioner and those s/he serves. Thus, professionals limit physical and social contact with clients, students and patients. While they engage in community interaction and social functions, they do not date or have intimate relations with those to whom they provide professional service. Lawyers sometimes know private details about a client's marital relationship. Doctors know intimate details about a patient's body. However, it is deemed inappropriate to greet a

1.0   Be A Competent Practitioner

client or patient with a hug or to touch them on the hand, shoulder or leg throughout a professional interaction.

Compare this to the norms of the Deaf community, in which greeting and leave-taking norms typically include a hug and sometimes a kiss on the cheek, similar to that found in some European cultures. The norms for attention-getting include touching the other person on the shoulder or arm and when seated beside each other, on the upper leg. Further, members of the Deaf community require that Sign Language professionals be a part of their social events so the community can monitor the linguistic, cultural, and attitudinal appropriateness and development of the professional.

This is based on a number of cultural norms and expectations, including the fact that the language of a minority group is the last bastion of power held by that group (Lane, 1984). In the eyes of the Deaf community, when individuals make money by using or teaching ASL, that person is accountable to their whole community. As a result, it is not enough to be a fluent signer, dynamic teacher, family member of a Deaf person, or above-average interpreter. One must be a part of the Deaf community,

1.0   Be A Competent Practitioner

interacting and socializing in appropriate ways, in order to get the "blessing" or informal endorsement of the community whose language they use in their professional endeavors.

Interpreters and teachers are expected to establish these interactions in the Deaf community before starting to practice professionally. Further, they are expected to maintain a presence and level of participation for as long as they work as interpreters or teachers of ASL or interpretation.

APPLYING THE STANDARDS

Armoire decided in high school that he wanted to work with individuals who were hearing and speech impaired. He studied speech therapy and received a BA degree in Communications Disorders from the local university. When he graduated, Armoire set up a private clinic where he worked with individuals with speech impairments. Some of his clients were deaf individuals, referred by parents, educational institutions and vocational rehabilitation counselors. Armoire does not sign and refuses to use the services of a Sign Language interpreter when working with clients because he focuses on speech reading and speaking skills.

REFLECTING ON ARMOIRE'S SITUATION: Armoire is not a Sign Language professional. Although he works with individuals who are Deaf and hard-of-hearing, Armoire's training, professional practice and related decisions and actions are based totally on the norms of professional behavior defined by the majority hearing community.

As a matter of fact, members of the Deaf community may refer to Armoire, his degree and work (and others like him) as "gold diggers' because they see no demonstration of real interest in or commitment to Deaf and hard-of-hearing clients beyond the scope of the office and invoices submitted.

1.0   Be A Competent Practitioner

APPLYING THE STANDARDS

Arabesque began signing while in high school after meeting some mainstreamed Deaf students, two of whom became close friends. Upon graduation, she enrolled in ASL courses in college and shared an apartment with her two high school friends. She began to learn about the grammar of ASL and the culture of the Deaf community.

While still a student, Arabesque began to interact socially with members of the Deaf community, attending holiday parties and events sponsored by various Deaf community organizations. A professor in her public speaking course asked her to make a presentation about Deaf culture and ASL since she was the only student in the class knowledgeable of those subjects.

Arabesque sensed that it would be more appropriate for a Deaf person to make this type of presentation, so she checked with her Deaf ASL instructor. Alerting the public speaking professor to her plans, she made arrangements for a member of the Deaf community to participate in the presentation.

REFLECTING ON ARABESQUE'S SITUATION: Arabesque is a Sign Language professional-in-training and she is already demonstrating awareness of and sensitivity to cross-cultural issues. In this event, Arabesque knew she was more knowledgeable about ASL and Deaf culture than other students in her class. She was also aware of the history of non-Deaf individuals speaking on behalf of individuals who are Deaf and the resulting sense of disenfranchisement by members of the Deaf community. By consulting with a reputable Deaf community member, Arabesque is beginning to form a habit of cultural awareness and is thus making first steps into informal Deaf community endorsement.

Arabesque was also sensitive to her non-Deaf college professor as she made arrangements to have the information presented to the class while helping the professor understand the issue of allowing a member of the language-culture group to share the information rather than having a hearing student do that.

1.0   Be A Competent Practitioner

1.4   Continue learning to ensure competent service and continued professional development.

This principle includes participating in advanced education, attending workshops and seminars, as well as staying current on recent research and standards of practice. A professional should be an active member in professional associations, attending meetings, participating in committee work, and reading professional literature.

Continued learning also includes interacting with other teachers or interpreters to reflect on one's professional decisions and practice in order to identify areas where changes may be needed. This may include working with a mentor or asking professional peers to observe your teaching or interpreting in order to provide feedback and suggestions that may advance your standard of practice. For interpreters, it may mean paying for a diagnostic evaluation to identify strengths and weaknesses in your interpretation in order to set goals for ongoing development.

Given the Deaf community's expectations of professionals, continued learning also includes demonstrated improvement in the use of ASL and in cultural awareness, sensitivity, and behaviors.

1.0   Be A Competent Practitioner

APPLYING THE STANDARDS

Dynomite and Ethellene are both certified Sign Language Interpreters, having taken and passed the national professional exam. They both began work as professional interpreters 18 years ago. Dynomite earned a Bachelor's degree at the local university while Ethellene completed a one-year interpreting course at the local community college. Dynomite continued her education part-time until she earned a Master's degree in Communications.

The interpreter association regularly sponsors workshops, as does the local interpreter preparation program. Ethellene finds the workshops time consuming and cumbersome. If the topic is interesting or the speaker is well known, Ethellene will attend a few hours — for a total of perhaps 4-hours per year. Dynomite attends every workshop and course she can in order to stay abreast of the changes and developments in the field — for a total of approximately 30-hours per year.

Recently Dynomite began work on a prior learning assessment portfolio that will be evaluated for academic credit. She hopes to be awarded a diploma in Sign Language interpretation. When someone questioned why she wanted to get an interpreting diploma — after all, she was already a certified interpreter — Dynomite responded that she felt it was important to keep learning, to stay up with changes in the field, and to model for other interpreters the need for ongoing learning.

REFLECTING ON DYNOMITE'S SITUATION: Dynomite is modeling the ideal regarding this ethical guideline. She realizes the dynamic nature of professional practice and the need to continually upgrade her knowledge and skills base. As a result, Dynomite's work continues to grow and improve as she incorporates new ideas and learning.

Ethellene, on the other hand, portrays a professional who is not abiding by the spirit of this ethical guideline. As a result, her work looks much the same today as it did ten years ago because her learning has plateaued.

Unfortunately, Deaf and hearing consumers are beginning to move Ethellene's name lower and lower on the list of preferred interpreters since her work is more and more inadequate to meet their needs.

1.0   Be A Competent Practitioner

1.5   Participate actively in applicable professional associations

Appropriate professional association(s) for Sign Language professionals include organizations for spoken and/or Sign Language interpreters, interpreter educators, Sign Language teachers, and associations of the Deaf (local and national), among others. The reason for this expectation is fairly obvious. Membership assumes support of the organization and that the member stays current with issues and developments in the field, attends professional conferences and stays in touch with colleagues in the field. Further, professional associations have the ability to review ethical concerns expressed by colleagues, consumers/clients and others, taking action as appropriate.

THE WORK ETHIC OF
SIGN LANGUAGE PROFESSIONALS

What is required of a Sign Language interpreter, ASL instructor or ASL/English interpreter educator in terms of work ethic? In this chapter, we will discuss standards regarding the level of industriousness, effort, energy and service required of a Sign Language professional. We have divided this chapter into the five sections in the Work Ethic guidelines.

1.0   Maintain Ethical Vigilance

It is not enough for a Sign Language professional to wait until an ethical concern is called to their attention. Vigilance implies a stance of alertness, being watchful for moral and ethical concerns, including the appearance of impropriety, and thinking critically before making decisions.

1.1   Regularly reflect on and think critically about professional decisions and actions in light of the Code of Ethics.

An ethical practitioner thinks about her/his professional performance, decisions and actions. At the end of each

1.0   Maintain Ethical Vigilance

day, s/he reflects on the day's work, evaluating the quality of the work performed and identifying strategies to improve their work and the quality of decisions made. Ethical vigilance includes the expectation that practitioners constantly seek ways to improve their professional performance.

1.2   Participate in collegial giving and receiving of constructive feedback with an eye to the healthy evolution of yourself and the profession.

Professionals often work in isolation, shielded from the evaluative eyes of peers. Because of this, ethical vigilance requires them to engage in ongoing dialogue and critical thinking with other practitioners regarding the variety of complex issues encountered in their day-to-day work. Only in this way can a professional be fully accountable for their work.

1.0   Maintain Ethical Vigilance

1.3   Take personal responsibility where inappropriate or unethical decisions and actions have been taken by you or your colleagues.

A professional is expected to take action in situations where there are concerns regarding her/his own ethical behavior. S/he should take responsibility where inappropriate or unethical decisions and actions have been taken, making apologies and amends as necessary and appropriate.

Finally, in a genuine spirit of concern and helpfulness, Sign Language professionals should tactfully approach colleagues whose decisions or behavior seems to have violated ethical standards. This is difficult for most practitioners. We don't want to be inappropriately judgmental, nor do we want to ignore the old adage "fools rush in where angels fear to tread" (Alexander Pope). But being a professional means we must take personal responsibility for both our own actions and our field of practice.

Professional responsibility includes a two-way giving and receiving of constructive feedback. When approached by

1.0   Maintain Ethical Vigilance

a colleague sharing her/his concerns about our decisions or behavior, a professional should avoid becoming defensive or personalizing the observations or comments made. The goal is to listen attentively, recognizing the value of the colleague's perspective and concerns — using the comments as a "mirror" to stimulate reflection on decisions and behavior.

Unfortunately, acting responsibly may sometimes include filing a formal grievance. This is often necessary when the preferred two-way interaction approach to problem solving fails.

APPLYING THE STANDARDS

Emmylou is a Sign Language interpreter. She is certified, holds a graduate degree, and teaches part-time in the local interpreter preparation program. Emmylou's interpreting contracts are primarily for ASL/English interpretation in mental health settings. She has been interpreting between a particular therapist and client for four years. After each session she reflects on the event, asking herself if she made appropriate choices and interpretations.

To date, she has been satisfied with the quality of her work. However, yesterday while the client was describing a hunting trip during which elk were shot, Emmylou began to have a personal reaction to the information. Although she was successful at conveying what the Deaf client was saying to the therapist, Emmylou had an overwhelming sense of blood — complete with the smell, color and texture.

1.0   Maintain Ethical Vigilance

During the debriefing session with the therapist after the client's departure, Emmylou mentioned her reaction to the therapist, stating that she would take it up with her own counselor. Once outside of the building, she called her therapist (whom she had not seen for several months) and made an appointment. She also scheduled dinner with a fellow interpreter who had served as a sounding board to Emmylou for several years.

With her own therapist, she began to seek some understanding as to what psychological or emotional buttons were pushed by the client's hunting story. These sessions will go on for a period of several weeks or months, providing Emmylou with a way to support her own emotional needs.

When she met with her interpreter friend, Emmylou explained what happened — while protecting any information that might betray who the Deaf client or therapist might have been. Her question was whether her colleague believed Emmylou could continue to work in this setting or if she should suggest to the therapist that another interpreter be introduced with the goal of eventually replacing Emmylou.

REFLECTING ON EMMYLOU'S SITUATION: Emmylou had developed a habit of reflecting on and reviewing her work and professional choices on a regular basis. When this incident occurred, she immediately sought experienced, yet neutral, professional opinions as to whether her personal reaction to the client's comments might prevent her from doing her job in a neutral and professional manner — thus putting her in some kind of ethical conflict. This type of careful, regular consideration of one's own work is one example of ethical vigilance.

2.0   Accept Professional Accountability

Professionals accept personal accountability for the decisions made and actions taken when providing service. This includes a number of areas such as representations of expertise and qualifications, as well as choice of apparel, schedule management, and preparation for work.

2.1   Claim or imply only those professional qualifications you actually possess.

Qualifications for professionals in most fields of practice have evolved over time and are clearly outlined for individuals seeking their services and for hiring agencies or institutions. Unfortunately, the fields of Sign Language interpretation, ASL instruction and interpreter education are relatively new. As a result, there is sometimes confusion or a lack of clarity regarding qualifications.

Because of this, it is incumbent on Sign Language professionals to clearly represent their qualifications. For example, a "certified (Sign Language) interpreter" refers only to an individual who has earned certification from either the Registry of Interpreters for the Deaf or the Association of Visual Language Interpreters of Canada. Thus, when

2.0   Accept Professional Accountability

employers and clients ask an interpreter if s/he is "certified,"
it is unethical for an individual to say "yes" when referring to
any other "certificate" — including certificates awarded for
participating in interpreting workshops or educational
programs. In areas where there are other credentials for
interpreters (state quality assurance system, employer
screening tool, etc.), an interpreter is ethically bound to
clarify what credentials they actually hold, rather than leaving
the impression that they hold certification from their
national organization.

There are some times when another person may
misrepresent your qualifications — perhaps when making an
introduction or when referring to you in some way. Ethical
standards require that a Sign Language professional correct
any misrepresentations of their qualifications by others. For
example, some Deaf community newsletters feature a
column welcoming new Deaf individuals to the community.
If they welcome a newcomer, noting that s/he has a Master's
degree in teaching ASL — when in fact the newcomer has
not completed that degree — a correction must be made. If
that misinformation is left uncorrected, it can be construed
that the newcomer willfully misrepresented her/his
credentials.

2.0   Accept Professional Accountability

APPLYING THE STANDARDS

Zenith received a certificate from the local interpreting program 18-months ago. She has worked almost exclusively in elementary and secondary educational settings where students use an English-based signing system. Because schools are closed during the summer, Zenith finds herself available to do some contract interpreting at that time.

The office of immigration contacted her one day and asked if she was certified as they needed her to interpret for an immigration hearing involving two Deaf individuals. Zenith was thrilled to be asked, stated that she held an interpreting certificate from the local college and accepted the job immediately. Upon arriving at the immigration office, she was escorted into an office where two immigration officers and two Deaf individuals from a third world country sat around a table.

The immigration officer asked a series of questions regarding the history of the two Deaf persons, including whether either individuals had ever ...

1) Attempted to enter the country before;
2) Had been evicted from any country;
3) Been convicted of a felony, etc.

Zenith simultaneously interpreted the questions as they were posed. When the Deaf individuals indicated lack of comprehension, Zenith signed more slowly and added inaudible English lip movements to assist them. More than once she observed the two Deaf individuals signing to each other in a way that she did not understand, but she thought nothing of it. Once all questions and answers had been interpreted, Zenith signed a form stating that she was a qualified interpreter and that the Deaf individuals had understood everything communicated.

REFLECTING ON ZENITH'S SITUATION   Zenith misrepresented her qualifications and education. This was probably done out of her eagerness to gain new interpreting experience. However her decision placed the welfare of two individuals at risk. As it turned out, the immigration office later learned that some of the information given in the interview was not true and attempted to evict the couple from the country for making false statements on their immigration documents.

In court, the defense case was based on the fact that an unqualified interpreter was used to interpret for the interview. Certified interpreters were subpoenaed to testify that they would not consider themselves qualified to interpret for this particular couple without the services of a Deaf (relay) interpreter. In the end, Zenith placed herself and her colleagues in an embarrassing adversarial situation and two innocent individuals were almost deported from the country.

2.0   Accept Professional Accountability

2.2 Information provided about a given situation or client, must:

a)   Be limited to your area of expertise;

b)   Conform to professional standards for confidentiality;

c)   Be accurate and unbiased; and

d)   Consist of factual, objective data.

Professionals are often asked to make statements to the media or to serve as "expert witnesses" in court or before a government or educational board. It is critical that Sign Language professionals ONLY provide information that is within their field of expertise. For example, while Sign Language interpreters constantly work to increase their knowledge about Deaf culture and American Sign Language, that fact alone does not qualify them as experts in those areas. An interpreter is an authority regarding the conveyance of information between English/ASL and hearing/Deaf cultures. When asked to present "expert" information on other areas, interpreters should clarify that they are not experts in those areas and suggest the names of others — often Deaf — who are, in fact, authorities in the areas being discussed.

2.0   Accept Professional Accountability

APPLYING THE STANDARDS

Popeye has Deaf relatives and began signing while quite young. He has been working as an interpreter for nine years and works in a variety of educational and community settings. During a recent court trial, Popeye was asked to appear as an expert witness on behalf of the defendant, a Deaf individual accused of a violent physical attack on his employer.

The lawyer explained that she wanted Popeye to discuss the reality of being Deaf in a hearing world, the level of stress and tension that could develop over time and the fact that many Deaf individuals act out physically when pushed long and hard enough. When Popeye said he didn't feel qualified to address those issues, the lawyer explained to him that his life-long involvement with Deaf persons, his Associate of Arts degree in sociology, and the fact that he had Deaf relatives qualified him as a expert in this matter.

REFLECTING ON POPEYE'S SITUATION: It is always flattering to have one's knowledge and experience valued by others. However it is critical that non-Deaf individuals respect the reality of oppression experienced by members of the Deaf community. In that history, hearing people made all of the decisions, speaking on behalf of Deaf individuals — usually without asking their opinions or confirming the accuracy of what they were saying.

Sign Language professionals must make ethical decisions within this historic framework. We must acknowledge that reading about the Deaf experience — even living with Deaf friends or family members does not qualify us to represent ourselves as experts in that area. Popeye made the right decision. He referred the lawyer to a qualified member of the Deaf community who was more appropriate as an expert witness.

2.0   Accept Professional Accountability

APPLYING THE STANDARDS

The local Kiwanis club has invited several individuals to make presentations at their monthly meeting about a variety of topics identified by their members. Ralph has invited Rhino — an ASL instructor and member of the Deaf community who works for Ralph — to speak about loss of hearing with old age and the variety of assistive devices available to help senior citizens as they face difficulties with hearing.

Rhino is feeling torn. He is hesitant to turn down his employer's request since he can use all the "brownie points" he can earn. After all, making his boss look good might eventually lead to that raise he has been wanting. At the same time, he knows nothing about late-life hearing loss, adaptive techniques or assistive listening devices appropriate for members of this population.

Rhino decides to collaborate with Benz, a fishing buddy of his who grew up with normal hearing and began losing his hearing several years ago. Rhino and Benz use some of the same devices to alert them to sound — a flashing light system attached to his telephone and door bell, as well as a visual fire alarm in his home. But Benz also depends on hearing aids, a voice carry-over telephone device rather than a TTY, and assistive listening devices more appropriate for those who lose their hearing later in life. Together, they made a dynamic presentation, each addressing those issues on which they were qualified to speak.

REFLECTING ON RHINO'S SITUATION: Rhino has demonstrated good ethical thinking and decision-making. He is aware of his own limitations and does not allow external pressure to push him into situations for which he is unqualified. By applying creative thinking, he has found a resolution for this situation which has a positive impact on everyone involved.

2.0   Accept Professional Accountability

When asked for a professional opinion, an individual must be able to separate negative or positive personal bias or subjective opinion from factual, objective data and observations.

APPLYING THE STANDARDS

Phroofroo is a teacher in an interpreting program with responsibility for courses related to interpersonal communication and cross-cultural dynamics. She was recently approached by a teacher who works in a school with a large Deaf/hard-of-hearing program. The teacher mentioned the name of one of Phroofroo's students and asked how the student was doing in the program.

Unfortunately, the student about whom the teacher inquired was one who had given Phroofroo a difficult time all semester. She never seemed to run out of questions or comments in class. She challenged Phroofroo on a regular basis, often arrived at class late, and never seemed to have homework ready to submit on time. Phroofroo responded to the question by rolling her eyes and letting out a big sign. "Oh my gosh!" she exclaimed, "What I'd give to get that one out of the program. She is a pain in the butt."

REFLECTING ON PHROOFROO'S SITUATION:
Unfortunately, Phroofroo's response is completely unprofessional and violates this ethical guideline. Phroofroo's response should have been something like, "Oh yes, so-and-so is a student in my cross-cultural communication course. All of the students in that course are struggling with some of the Deaf-hearing issues they will encounter as interpreters." The content of this response is factual and devoid of bias or negative personal judgments.

2.0   Accept Professional Accountability

One ethical standard common to all professions is that of
confidentiality. While it is sometimes necessary to consult
with another professional about a patient or client, the
standard of professional communication incorporates the
exclusion of names or identifying information to protect the
privacy of those receiving professional services.

Sign Language professionals need to be hyper-vigilant in
regard to compliance with this ethical standard due to the
size and nature of the Deaf community. A member of the
Deaf community can identify another member of the
community with very little identifying information. For
example, in some situations the following details could
betray the identity of an interpreting client:

- Redheaded male with moustache;

- Single Mom with two girls;

- Moved here from (such-and-such town);

- Deaf husband, hearing wife.

2.0   Accept Professional Accountability

Thus, there is a need to handle with greatest care any communication about one's work.

APPLYING THE STANDARDS

Neopreme is an ASL/English interpreter and a single mother of two children ages 8 and 10. She has decided that she wants her children to have natural exposure to ASL so they have an opportunity to develop bilingual skills. As a result, she has a Deaf baby sitter who watches her children when she must work evening and weekend hours.

She knows the rules about confidentiality required of Sign Language professionals. However, she needs to leave the baby-sitter information about how to contact her in the event of an emergency. She typically leaves the phone number, location, and name of contact person at that location.

When she gets home, she spends some time chatting with her babysitter before the sitter leaves. On occasion, she "slips" and says something about seeing Gilligan or MaryAnne at the AA meeting but she doesn't worry about it since she assumes her babysitter will keep things confidential.

REFLECTING ON NEOPREME'S SITUATION: Neopreme's desire to have her children learn ASL in a natural way is commendable. However, she is compromising her clients' confidentiality in several ways.

A better choice might be to carry a cell phone and portable TTY or a pager so the babysitter can contact her but is not privy to information that might reveal the clients and settings in which Neoprene is working.

3.0   Present A Professional Image & Presence

Professionals are held to certain norms and expectations regarding personal appearance, timeliness and entering the sphere of work adequately prepared for the task.

3.1   Comply with the norms for personal appearance when functioning in a professional role.

This standard includes expectation of a neat and tidy personal appearance. While professional practitioners are not expected to look like they just walked off the pages of a fashion magazine, there is an expectation that clothes will be clean, neatly pressed, and free from tears, missing buttons, and dangling hem lines. Clothing should not be too tight and hemlines should not be too short. Generally speaking, athletic shorts, tank tops, running suits and other such casual apparel are inappropriate. Professionals should consider the visual background created by the color and pattern of their clothing in order to avoid visual fatigue on the part of their clients/students. Shoes should be polished, free from mud and other debris, and appropriate to the setting.

3.0   Present A Professional Image & Presence

Hair should be neat, clean and arranged in a non-distracting style. If a beard or moustache is worn, care should be taken to insure that it is neatly trimmed. A Sign Language professional must be sure that hair style and facial hair not obscure critical facial features — lips, cheeks, eyebrows, etc. — that convey grammatical information in ASL.

Likewise fingernails should be clean and trimmed to an appropriate length. Nails that are too long result in inaccurately formed handshapes and cause visual distraction. If nail polish is used, a neutral color near the shade of skin tone is recommended. Bright and/or iridescent colors should be avoided.

> "Language is the expression of thought. Every time you speak, your mind is on parade."

3.0   Present A Professional Image & Presence

APPLYING THE STANDARDS
Oak lives on a small acreage just outside of town. He has chickens, a few goats, and a horse. Last Thursday he was scheduled to provide platform interpretation for the plenary session of a large convention. He did not have any other assignments on Thursday, so he spent the day doing chores around the farm — collecting eggs, feeding the animals, planting some vegetables in the garden.
Awareness of time escaped him. When he realized he was late, he washed his face and hands, put on clean clothes and slipped back into the same shoes he had been wearing all day. Oak didn't notice that they had chicken droppings and mud on them. He arrived just as the session was starting. His team interpreter, Cedar, noticed his shoes and jotted a quick note for him to read when they exchanged positions. Then she took her place on the platform. When Oak sat down, he saw Cedar's note, looked at his shoes and immediately went to the Men's room where he cleaned his shoes. He then returned to the convention and resumed his work.
REFLECTING ON OAK'S SITUATION: Ideally, Oak would have checked his personal appearance prior to leaving home where he would have realized the problem and fixed it. However this didn't happen. It would help Oak and all Sign Language professionals if they do a quick check of their appearance before entering the site where they will be working. By slipping into the washroom, one can take quick inventory — hair, face, hands, nails, clothing of upper body, clothing of lower body, shoes.
In this incident, Oak and Cedar worked together in a professional manner. Cedar was not negative or accusatory when writing her note to Oak. Likewise, Oak did not personalize Cedar's suggestion or become defensive. He accepted the observation and took personal action to remedy the situation.

3.0   Present A Professional Image & Presence

3.2   Come to work prepared to provide the highest quality of professional service.

Spontaneity and the ability to improvise are nice skills to have. However a professional does not enter the arena of professional practice unprepared. Teachers are expected to have lesson plans, complete with specific learning objectives and related learning activities prepared in advance of each class. Likewise, interpreters have a responsibility to gather certain information in advance (e.g. names of individuals involved including sign names, instructor handouts, chapters being taught, words to songs, etc).

A critical characteristic that complements preparation is flexibility. As another old paraphrase goes, "the best laid plans of mice and men go oft astray" (Robert Burns). In the face of reality, things rarely go as expected and professionals must maintain their composure as they "roll with the punches."

Students and clients have a right to expect their teacher or interpreter to come to work rested, physically well and psychologically focused on the task at hand. Personal problems must be put aside when providing a professional service. Further, it is inappropriate to discuss with students

3.0   Present A Professional Image & Presence

or clients personal problems, physical illness, injuries, or grievances toward others. If one is too ill or distracted by personal issues to provide quality service, s/he should take sick leave and arrange for a substitute teacher/interpreter.

Finally, professionals do their best to be on time. Interpreters and itinerant teachers should schedule their commitments in such a way that they do not cause the delay or cancellation of a class or interpreted interaction. Personal commitments are not routinely allowed to interfere with timeliness.

APPLYING THE STANDARDS

Thyme is a busy professional. She does freelance interpreting 20 – 30 hours per week, in addition to teaching part-time in the interpreter education program. She is also a single Mom to Adam, age 5, and Eve, age 3, and she sells beauty products on the side.

Today was fairly typical of Thyme's daily routine. She didn't get to bed until well past midnight because she was busy doing laundry and packing lunches for the children. This morning she was up and showered by 6:30, after which she woke, bathed, dressed and fed the children. At 7:45 she put the kids in their car seats and left for the daycare center. She was running about 15-minutes late. Predictably, Eve had a hard time saying goodbye and she was not able to leave the daycare center until 8:20.

She knew she would be late to her 8:30 interpreting appointment — but what could she do? She fought through morning rush hour and ran hurriedly into her appointment at 8:50, apologizing to the anxious participants and making up an excuse about the car not starting.

Since the 8:30 meeting could not start until 8:50, IT RAN OVER. This made Thyme late to her 10:30 appointment, a meeting that also ran past time. Thyme rushed out of the 10:30 appointment and started looking for some place to stop and grab a quick bite to eat (she is hypoglycemic and it is important that she keep her blood sugar level). This caused her to arrive at

3.0   Present A Professional Image & Presence

her 12:45 class at 1:15, just as students were getting ready to give up on her and leave.

Thyme had been busy since her last class and had not really prepared her lesson so she used the first part of the class session to address some ancillary questions and topics. At break, she ran up to the office and copied part of an article she happened to have in her briefcase. She did not take time to note the source of the article. The copy machine was not working well, copies were blurred and hard to read — but at least it was *something* for the students.

After class, Thyme started for her 3:00 p.m. interpreting appointment. She had a few minutes to spare so she dropped off some beauty products at two locations. This short detour caused her to arrive at her next appointment at exactly 3:00 p.m., leaving no time to familiarize herself with clients, interpreting partner, or the topic being addressed. In spite of that, this session went well, with each interpreter working 20-25 minute turns.

Thyme realized that she would be in the "off" or "supporting" position for the final segment of the assignment. Since she would face a late charge from her children's daycare canter if they were not picked up before 5:00 p.m., she told her interpreting partner that she would leave the assignment early — leaving her partner to work alone for that last segment.

REFLECTING ON THYME'S SITUATION: If this is typical, Thyme's schedule is out of control. She is not behaving in a responsible, ethical or professional manner. Some things that would help Thyme include:

1)   Allow more travel and transition time. If she is typically unable to get the children to daycare on time or if the children regularly require a bit of "good-bye time," Thyme should not accept appointments before 9:00 a.m. As she schedules appointments, she needs to be sensitive to the time of day and distance involved so she can more accurately predict travel time.

2)   Prepare a bag lunch or healthy snacks she can eat or drink regularly throughout the day, avoiding the need to look frantically for food when the low blood sugar kicks in. Extremes in blood sugar result in poor concentration and low energy, as well as being a threat to the health.

3)   Get a cell phone so she can notify people when she is unavoidably delayed. This should not become the "norm" but should be the exception to the rule.

4)   Thyme needs to schedule enough time to prepare for her classes and for assignments. It is not fair to her students or clients for her to "fly by the seat of her britches." If she is not able to do this, she has a professional responsibility to turn down some interpreting requests and/or to stop teaching part-time.

3.0   Present A Professional Image & Presence

3.3   Services rendered, including materials used, should reflect professional standards and quality.

It is not enough to "do one's best" or to provide "adequate" service. Both the mainstream and Deaf communities have a right to expect — at the very least — a minimum standard of excellence from practitioners. Peers also expect the work of colleagues to reflect professional criteria.

All forms of communication should reflect a professional standard. Letters, invoices, resumés and other written documents should reflect proper format, content, and spelling. Teachers are expected to prepare for classes in advance so their materials and handouts are free from misspelled terms, information lacking proper citation, etc. Interpreters are expected to have a date book with them when they go to an appointment, rather than jotting down dates and times of future appointments on scraps of paper which may be lost or forgotten.

3.0 Present A Professional Image & Presence

3.4 Take personal responsibility for quality of service provision.

Professionals arrive at assignments on time. "On time" is defined as at least 10 — 15 minutes before the scheduled beginning. For teachers, this allows time to change room set up if needed, place audio-visual equipment in appropriate locations, pre-set videotapes, etc. For interpreters, this allows time to determine communication compatibility, meet new clients/consumers, check out physical space, make placement decisions, etc.

Interpreters in private practice and contract teachers working at different sites must be careful not to schedule appointments/classes too close together, taking into consideration the reality of travel time at various hours of the day. A pattern of absence or tardiness is unacceptable and reflects badly on the profession. On the rare occasion when a professional is unavoidably delayed, s/he will call ahead and let people know an estimated time of arrival. If a professional is sick or injured, s/he will make arrangements for a substitute to provide service in her/his place. In the event the teacher/interpreter cannot find a substitute, s/he will need to go to the appointment/class and provide service, unless to do so would endanger the health of others.

4.0   Fees for Professional Services

As Sign Language professionals, we enjoy working with people — teaching them a new language or skill, mediating communication between two language and culture groups. However, since few of us are independently wealthy, we must also receive remuneration for our services. Like other professional groups, we need to approach this part of our practice in a principled way — sensitive to our clients' needs and ability to pay while respecting the value of the service we provide.

4.1   Hold the needs of clients/consumers primary when making decisions regarding fees for service.

Professionals in all fields have ways of establishing "sliding scale" fees in order to make their services accessible to all members of the public sector. This is particularly true of Sign Language interpreters, whose services are sometimes so critical that they must be purchased, whether or not the fee is reasonable and appropriate.

4.0   Appropriate Fees for Professional Services

APPLYING THE STANDARDS

Daffodil is a freelance ASL instructor, currently teaching classes at three different area colleges. She was recently contacted by the City-Wide College and asked to teach an ASL course there on Tuesday evenings.

The pay at City-Wide is more per hour than that paid at the other three schools and Daffodil could use the additional income. However, when she figured the travel time from her late Tuesday afternoon class and the proposed new class, she realized she would not be able to get to the City-Wide campus prior to class time. In addition, this is a class that Daffodil has never taught before so she would need more preparation time. Daffodil would like to take the new class but she is concerned about (1) adequate preparation and study time for this new course and (2) ability to arrive at class early.

Daffodil decides to meet with the program coordinator at City-Wide and discuss options. For example, if the class can be offered on Wednesday evening, Daffodil would have adequate preparation and travel time. She knows that if no compromise can be made, she will need to turn down the class and recommend someone else.

REFLECTING ON DAFFODIL'S SITUATION: Daffodil is modeling appropriate thinking and decision-making. She is holding her professional commitment and responsibility paramount while acknowledging and balancing her skills, ability and personal needs. Daffodil dismissed the following options because she felt they were not ethical:

1) Taking the class and announcing to the students on the first night that the start time had been changed to thirty minutes later;

2) Asking a friend to "cover" for her and take the last hour of her Tuesday afternoon class each week so she can slip off to City-Wide early;

3) Dismissing her Tuesday afternoon class early every week in order to arrive at City-Wide on time.

4.0   Appropriate Fees for Professional Services

4.2   Be aware of and sensitive to professional and cultural norms regarding fees for professional service.

In establishing fees for professional services, practitioners should consider:

a)   The source of payment;

b)   The financial status of payer;

c)   Local cost of living; and

d)   Professional fee standards.

In the event that the established fee structure is out of reach for an individual, assistance should be provided in finding comparable services at an acceptable cost.

APPLYING THE STANDARDS

OliveOyle lives in a large metropolitan area where the cost of living is fairly high. She is a recent graduate from the interpreting program at the local community college. While in the program, she did a research project in which she learned that freelance rates ranged from $25 - $35 in her community, depending on experience, education and certification.

Immediately after graduation, she printed business cards and began to solicit work as a private practice interpreter. She set her rates at $30 per hour with a 2-hour minimum. When approached by a member of the Deaf community

4.0   Fees for Professional Services

and asked to interpret for a 20-minute discussion with his neighbor, OliveOyle reminded him that she would have to be paid since she was now a professional and it was not appropriate to donate her time. The Deaf community member looked a bit surprised — or was it anger? — and asked how much. She quoted her standard rates. The neighbor decided he could get along without an interpreter.

REFLECTING ON OLIVEOYLE'S SITUATION OliveOyle has made several errors in judgment in this situation. While she made her decision about fees for service based on an assessment of standard practice in her community, OliveOyle failed to take into consideration her lack of experience both in the Deaf community and as an interpreter. She also seems unaware of her "reciprocity pool" responsibility to the Deaf community as a novice interpreter.

A more appropriate approach would have been for OliveOyle to set her initial fees below those of experienced practitioners. For example, she may have set her fees at $15 per hour for the first six-months and raised her fees to $17.50 for the next six months. In this way, she is acknowledging that the value of her service is less than that of more experienced practitioners.

Members of the Deaf community are expected to participate in the reciprocity pool, especially outsiders who have received the gift of ASL. OliveOyle would have been demonstrating greater sensitivity to her role in the Deaf community and appreciation for the gift of ASL upon which her new career was based if she had volunteered to provide 20-minutes of interpretation as requested. If Olive has concerns about 20-minutes becoming 2-hours, she needs to set up a clear understanding about how much time she can actually provide some volunteer interpreting. (NOTE: All professionals volunteer a certain amount of their time and services to their community. This is referred to as *pro bono* work and normally represents a significant contribution of time and talent. A brief 20-minute gift of time does not fall into the category of *pro bono* work.)

4.0   Appropriate Fees for Professional Services

APPLYING THE STANDARD

Diction moved to Podunk from a large metropolitan area a few months ago. In the city, she was charging $65 per hour for interpreting in mental health and legal settings. She sees no reason to lower her rates now that she has relocated. She believes that her skills and experience are as valuable in Podunk as they were in the city — perhaps even more so since she is now the only certified interpreter in a 300-mile radius.

The court clerk is not at all happy. She has been paying court interpreters $35 per hour. Now all of the interpreters want the same wage as Diction.

David Deaf contacted Diction, asking her to interpret for a traffic court appearance and an appointment with his family lawyer to draw up a will. David explained that he would be paying Diction himself since the city/county and family lawyer would not provide an interpreter. Diction accepted the work.

When David got an invoice a few weeks later for $65 per hour, the retired brick layer nearly had a heart attack. Surely this was a mistake. He contacted Diction and asked for clarification. She confirmed that the fee was $65 per hour — that was her legal fee, period. Further, she expected payment within 30-days.

REFLECTING ON DICTION'S SITUATION: Diction is not behaving in an appropriate professional manner in this situation. Fees should have been discussed and agreed to in advance of service. Further, Diction needs to adjust her hourly rate to that which is commonly found in and around Podunk. If she had checked, she would have learned that the most expensive lawyer and psychiatrist in town only charge $50 per hour. Her fee of $65 is beyond the range of professionals in that geographic area — probably due to the lower cost of living in the region. In addition, interpreters typically charge less per hour/day when a Deaf client is bearing the cost. This is done partially to reflect "reciprocity pool" norms and partly in response to the fact that a majority of Deaf individuals are under-employed and underpaid due to ongoing discrimination in the work place.

Finally, other payment options include bartering or reciprocity, as well as a payment plan. These other possibilities should be considered when a Deaf client is paying for services directly.

THE ETHICS OF PROFESSIONAL RELATIONSHIPS

Relationships develop between Interpreters, ASL instructors and ASL/English interpreter educators and their students, clients and members of the public in a variety of professional settings. Sign Language professionals have a responsibility to maintain high standards of conduct in these interactions. Further, ASL and interpreting teachers are in a unique position of modeling ethical behavior, decision-making and cross-cultural sensitivity for their students.

The information in this chapter, relates to the following professional relationships:

1. Conduct toward clients/students with whom the professional interacts directly;

2. Behavior toward the institution within which the service is performed; and

3. Interactions with the Deaf and professional communities.

1.0 Establish & Maintain Professional Boundaries

Professionals are expected to establish and maintain appropriate boundaries between themselves and their students and/or clients, allowing friendly, supportive interactions while avoiding behaviors that may threaten (or be perceived by others as threatening) one's objectivity or professional judgment.

The definition of appropriate boundaries in the majority community is typically "involved but separate." In other words, professionals establish fairly wide physical, social, and psychological barriers between themselves and those to whom they provide professional services in order to maintain objectivity and professional judgment. Evidence of this includes such examples as:

1)   We do not typically greet our dentist with a hug;

2)   We rarely attend a holiday party with our doctor or therapist; and

3)   We normally refer to professionals by title (Dr. White, Ms. Brown, etc).

The use of titles creates a psychological boundary and reinforces established hierarchies in our society. Lack of social interaction reflects the fact that the majority community has a large number of members and therefore

1.0 Establish & Maintain Professional Boundaries

an abundance of resources. The community is large enough that one does not have to use a personal friend as their physician or attorney.

This is not the reality for members of some minority communities. When a community is small, members are often required to assume multiple roles. These phenomena are also seen in rural communities. This explains why the Deaf community expects ASL/English interpreters and teachers of ASL and interpretation to establish community connections as discussed in Chapter Four.

However, it is important that Sign Language professionals consider the ways in which appropriate boundaries can be established and maintained to protect both the professional and her/his clientele.

1.1 Limit physical contact with your students/clients.

Greeting and leave-taking behaviors must be modified, based on the setting and the relationship between the Sign Language professional and the individual s/he is greeting. When greeting Deaf friends and acquaintances at a Deaf

1.0 Establish & Maintain Professional Boundaries

community gathering, an interpreter will typically follow the norm of exchanging a hug and perhaps a kiss on the cheek. The same interpreter meeting the same Deaf community member in a setting where there is a professional relationship (interpreter/client) would generally refrain from using a Deaf cultural greeting behavior. Several factors are at work here, including the need to:

- Establish a professional relationship with the Deaf community member (overtly "change hats," as it were);

- Avoid the appearance of bias or lack of neutrality in the eyes of hearing clients.

If a hug is used for a greeting, it is modified in length and degree of physical contact to support the cross-cultural needs mentioned above.

Sign Language professionals need to monitor their choices when taking a break from teaching or interpreting. A teacher may take a break with a group of students but should avoid regularly taking a break with a single student or the same group of students. For example, if there is a subset of students who smoke on break, it is not appropriate for the teacher to consistently take a break with that group of students during or after class even if the teacher is a smoker.

1.0 Establish & Maintain Professional Boundaries

This could create the appearance of favoritism or lack of neutrality.

During breaks in long interpreting assignments, an interpreter should be careful not to take breaks with either the Deaf or hearing client(s) if there is any type of adversarial relationship or power differentiation between Deaf and hearing clients.

We must also be cautious about private meetings with students/clients. Teachers meeting one-on-one with a student should consider leaving their office or classroom door open to avoid allegations of inappropriate behavior. If an interpreter needs to meet with a client in advance of an interpreted event, s/he should consider meeting in a public setting such as a restaurant or coffee shop rather than meeting in someone's home. Likewise, it is not wise to meet students/clients for private social interludes.

Care should also be taken regarding where discussions of a professional nature take place. An interpreter should not discuss an interpreted event nor should a teacher disclose a student's grades or classroom performance where others can eavesdrop on the discussion. It is particularly important to avoid discussions of this nature when at a Deaf community event.

1.0 Establish & Maintain Professional Boundaries

APPLYING THE STANDARDS

Aardvark is Deaf, as are her parents. She has been hired to teach ASL on a full-time basis at the local college. She enjoys working with students and is an excellent teacher. She knows it is her responsibility to be a culture guide to students, as well as a language teacher. She incorporates Deaf culture norms of greeting, physical contact, eye contact and physical space when interacting with her students.

After six months, two hearing students — both male — filed a sexual harassment complaint against Aardvark, alleging sexual touching and favoritism toward certain students.

REFLECTING ON AARDVARK'S SITUATION: This is a classic example of a cross-cultural/cross-communication dilemma. These students have misunderstood the hug-greeting, sustained eye contact and physical touch attention-getting behaviors as intimate and sexual in nature.

Aardvark must remember that she works in a hearing institution that functions on mainstream institution norms. She must educate both students and the administration about deafness and some of the behaviors and norms that vary from the mainstream. At the same time, Aardvark must modify her interactions with students, colleagues and others in this setting to conform to mainstream professional expectations.

1.0 Establish & Maintain Professional Boundaries

APPLYING THE STANDARDS

Quark is an interpreter who interacts with members of the Deaf community on a regular basis. At the Halloween party last week, he greeted others in attendance with the typical hug and kiss greeting of the Deaf community. Among others, he greeted and chatted with Quirk and his partner Pansie.

Today when Quark met Quirk and Pansie at the courthouse where he was scheduled to interpret a legal hearing in front of a Judge, he nodded at them with a friendly smile and shook hands in greeting. When the legal hearing was over, Pansie thanked Quark for interpreting and began to move toward him to exchange a (deaf culture appropriate) brief hug. Quark turned his body slightly, which preempted the hug and patted Pansie on the back before physically moving away from her — just enough to avert the hug but not so much his movement would be misinterpreted as unfriendly and cold.

REFLECTING ON QUARK'S SITUATION: This scenario provides a good model of how interpreters modify their physical interactions as they move between cultural events. Quark was culturally appropriate in a Deaf predominant setting, yet was sensitive to appearance of even quick greetings that might be misunderstood in a different setting.

1.0 Establish & Maintain Professional Boundaries

1.2   Monitor your social interactions with students/clients.

Due to the Deaf cultural norms and expectations, there are times when Sign Language professionals are required to attend events and socialize with Deaf clients. In addition, ASL teachers will require students to attend various Deaf community social functions. As a result, it is imperative for both students and professionals to monitor their actions in these settings. The goal is to remain friendly, approachable and sociable while maintaining appropriate demeanor and separation from our students/clients.

For example, we should not give students/clients a ride to an appointment or event, nor should we regularly accept a ride in a student's/client's car. In addition to issues of appearance, there are legal liabilities to be considered.

Sign Language professionals sometimes have long-running contact with students and clients. For example, an ASL teacher may have contact with a student from their first Sign language course through her/his becoming an interpreter. Questions sometimes arise regarding holidays, birthdays, weddings and births. As a rule, professionals do not give or

1.0 Establish & Maintain Professional Boundaries

accept expensive or personal gifts on any occasion. Giving or receiving a card or a small, impersonal gift is acceptable on significant occasions but should not be encouraged. It is also acceptable if a group contributes to a gift at the end of an ongoing professional relationship. For example, students may contribute to the purchase of a small item such as a book or videotape for an instructor at the end of a course of study. When an interpreter moves from the community, a group of individuals may go together to purchase a farewell gift, particularly if that interpreter has had some kind of ongoing professional relationship with that group of individuals.

When socializing at community events, Sign Language professionals can have a good time while maintaining a certain amount of professional decorum. One should not engage in telling offensive jokes or engaging in physical activities that might put her/his judgment, maturity or credibility in question. For example, it is never appropriate to get intoxicated on alcohol or drugs in the presence of students or clients of your professional services.

1.0 Establish & Maintain Professional Boundaries

APPLYING THE STANDARDS

BluByrd is a Sign Language interpreter. She commits two weekends every month to "on call" duty for three local hospitals. Last week she was called to the emergency room shortly after midnight. The Deaf patient arrived by ambulance a few minutes after BluByrd arrived. Several hours later, the Deaf individual was released and told to go home. She asked the nurse how she could get home. The nurse shrugged her shoulders and said, "That's your problem" and walked off.

Uncertainty shone from the patient's eyes. She looked at BluByrd and said, "Can you take me home?" BluByrd replied, "No, I'm sorry. I can't — interpreter rules" but she went on to suggest a cab, bus or walking home if it was not too distant. The Deaf individual remarked that she had no money for a cab, the bus didn't run that late at night, and she didn't feel safe walking home at that time of night. BluByrd asked if anyone was at home, to which the Deaf client said, "Yes, my roommate." BluByrd asked, "Could you take a cab and get your roommate to pay when you get home?"

The Deaf individual's eyes widened. "Good idea!" She then asked BluByrd to interpret a call to the roommate to verify that s/he had money and was willing to pay the cab. Then she interpreted a call for the cab. BluByrd left the hospital before the cab arrived, wishing the client good health.

REFLECTING ON BLUBYRD'S SITUATION: BluByrd made a good decision. Had she taken the Deaf individual in her personal car and there had been an auto accident or a medical emergency on the part of the client, BluByrd may have been facing serious legal liability.

In addition, agreeing to take this client home might put BluByrd in an unsafe situation — not knowing what might be waiting on the other end of that ride. Further, going through the exercise of asking questions and making suggestions, gave her client an opportunity to learn more about the system, how to solve problems and perhaps will give her skills that will empower her to make better choices in the future.

1.0 Establish & Maintain Professional Boundaries

APPLYING THE STANDARDS

Pepin is an ASL teacher. One part of his course outline requires students to attend a certain number of Deaf community events, collect some type of "proof of attendance" (ticket stub, program, etc.) and write a summary of their experiences. On a weekly basis, Pepin announces different upcoming events where students could go to complete the required number of hours of community interaction.

As a result, when Pepin attends community events, he is careful to guard his behavior. If he drinks alcohol, he does so moderately. He does not participate in the use of drugs before or during the event. He chats with friends and engages in friendly "one-ups-manship" with pals. When one of his students asks him to dance with her, he tactfully declines — unless it is a line dance or something where there is no "partnering" in the dance pattern.

REFLECTING ON PEPIN'S SITUATION: Pepin knows his students must interact in the community if they are to ever master the language and learn the subtle nuances of the culture. At the same time, he is sometimes a bit regretful that his professional life and his social community cannot be more separate. However, he has ways to balance his personal needs and his professional responsibilities.

For example, there are some community events the he does not announce to students — sometimes because that particular event would not be appropriate for hearing students and sometimes because he wants to attend without the constraints placed on him by having students present. He also gathers with friends in smaller groupings at various homes. Others at these small events are often professionals, as well, people meeting their social needs away from the watchful eye of students/clients.

1.0 Establish & Maintain Professional Boundaries

1.3   Maintain psychological separation between yourself and the students/clients with whom you work.

Sign Language professionals often have access to personal, confidential information about their client/ student that occasionally creates the aura of intimacy. Once again, there is a cultural difference here. Deaf culture typically defines a person by who they know in the community. As a result, Sign Language professionals are expected to share more personal information in Deaf settings than is appropriate in mainstream settings. However, there is still a limit. It is important that one's consumers do not become part of one's personal support network. That is why professionals do not confide in or share unnecessary personal information with students/clients. For example, the fact that the teacher's child had an accident or their home was burglarized should not become the impromptu topic of discussion. Rather, class time should be spent focusing on the learning objectives appropriate to the curriculum. If the child's accident or the burglary is so traumatic that the teacher is unable to do this, s/he should arrange for a substitute teacher in order to ensure that the students receive the education for which they have paid.

1.0 Establish & Maintain Professional Boundaries

It goes without saying that an ethical professional never dates or has a sexual relationship with someone to whom they are providing professional service. This same principle also applies to members of the student's/client's immediate family. Likewise, it is not generally appropriate for a teacher to teach her/his own family member or for an interpreter to interpret for someone with whom s/he has a close emotional bond.

APPLYING THE STANDARDS

Lobelia is a freelance interpreter. Last month she spent three days interpreting for a Deaf client as she went through a variety of medical interviews and physical, mental and occupational stamina examinations. This exam is being done as part of a personal injury lawsuit and has been ordered by the opposing lawyer, attempting to demonstrate that the Deaf individual is fully capable of returning to work. The days were long and grueling, going from 8:00 a.m. to 4:30 and 5:00 p.m. Lobelia met her client in the lobby of the building each morning so they entered and left the medical office together each day. They also went to lunch together each noon and took their breaks together. During the various examinations and interviews, the Deaf client responded with obvious pain and discomfort. As a part of her interpretation, Lobelia included vocal affect that reflected that pain.

1.0 Establish & Maintain Professional Boundaries

Three weeks later, the Deaf client met with her attorney who was quite upset about a letter he had received from the medical examination. The doctors noted that the interpreter was biased in favor of the Deaf woman. "The interpreter exaggerated her vocal intonation to create an impression of great pain," the report stated. The lawyer was concerned that the Deaf client's case may have been seriously damaged.

REFLECTING ON LOBELIA'S SITUATION: Whereas Deaf clients generally understand the role of an interpreter, hearing clients have often had no such experience and are more likely to misinterpret what they see going on. Lobelia was correct in taking on the vocal affect to reflect the pain expressed by the Deaf client. Her professional association could write a letter supporting her professional choices and explaining typical protocol for clarification to the lawyer and the medical personnel involved in this case.

Interpreters are trained to spend some time with a Deaf client in order to build trust, verify ease of communication, etc. However, in an adversarial relationship this behavior may cast doubt in the minds of other professionals in the setting. Maintaining proper social and psychological boundaries, equivalent for all clients is critical. Distancing herself from the Deaf client completely may leave the client confused and hurt. Spending every minute of "down time" with the Deaf client will probably be misinterpreted by hearing professionals as a lack of neutrality.

This is a situation where Lobelia might have shared one break each day with the Deaf client, taking her lunch alone and being sure to enter the medical office alone sometimes — rather than in the company of the Deaf client each time.

1.0 Establish & Maintain Professional Boundaries

1.4   Do not manipulate a work situation for personal benefit and/or potential harm to clients/students.

Because we are in a position of trust and power, professional practitioners have the ability and opportunity to manipulate or influence some work-related elements. We must be careful to avoid doing so for personal benefit. Professionals always hold the interests of their clients above those of their own.

For example, it is unethical to allow your financial situation to influence decisions regarding accepting work for which you may not be qualified or which may result in a schedule that precludes timeliness and appropriate preparation. It is also inappropriate to convince clients to manipulate the time or date of an event solely so you can get another job under your belt. The exception to this rule is when the client specifically requests that you interpret the next appointment to maintain continuity.

1.0 Establish & Maintain Professional Boundaries

APPLYING THE STANDARDS

Peppermint teaches full-time in a Sign Language interpreting program. He also does a lot of freelance interpreting. He is expected to be on campus 30-35 hours per week, teaching, advising, planning, marking papers and participating in departmental committees.

Last month, Peppermint received a call from a large multi-level marketing company asking him to interpret a three-day meeting — Wednesday through Friday from 9:00 a.m. to 4:30 p.m. each day. They offered him $1,000 per day and guaranteed they would book a second interpreter to work with him.

Peppermint accepted the job offer without a moment's hesitation. He knew this type of meeting would be "public" and that he should have no problem getting permission for his students to attend in order to observe the interpreters. The fact that students would miss 15-hours of instruction didn't seem to enter his mind.

At the next class, Peppermint excitedly told students their class schedule was being changed in order to accommodate a field trip to observe interpreters. As a result, he cancelled an exam that had originally been planned for one of those days.

REFLECTING ON PEPPERMINT'S SITUATION:
Peppermint has made an unethical decision. He has manipulated the class schedule and the students' learning plan in order to make a quick $ 3,000. In addition, he is being paid by the college and by the multi-level marketing company for work on the same days at the same times. This is fraudulent behavior and could result in Peppermint being fired from the college.

If Peppermint wants to do the freelance work, he should speak with his supervisor and request vacation leave for those days. In addition, substitute teachers should be located to teach the classes Peppermint will be missing.

1.0 Establish & Maintain Professional Boundaries

Likewise, teachers should not give students assignments from which they will gain personal benefit. For example, it is unethical for a teacher to require students to meet at a mall for class, ostensibly because s/he plans to teach locatives and classifiers, although the real reason is because the teacher needs to do some shopping. In the same way, an interpreter educator should not arrange for students to observe her/his work as an interpreter, witness or speaker in a public setting solely because the educator has made a commitment to this other work in conflict with class time.

2.0 Guard Client's Personal Dignity and Right to Self-Determination/Empowerment

Professionals are expected to relate with respect toward the individuals with whom they work, both clients and colleagues. This includes being respectful of and sensitive to the uniqueness and value of each client and/or student regardless of geographic, economic, educational, social position, or other factors. Each person with whom we work

2.0   Guard Client's Personal Dignity and Right to Self-Determination/Empowerment

has her/his unique style of communication and personal history. Each student masters skills and knowledge according to their own learning style. It is incumbent on the professional to respect and work effectively within the framework of this individuality.

It is critical that we avoid all forms of stereotyping and discrimination (racism, sexism, audism,[1] ageism, etc.). Teachers need to reflect on the nature and content of examples, anecdotes, and jokes used in the classroom to ensure that they are free of any bias or prejudice.

Further, it is unprofessional and unethical to condone or engage in deliberate or repeated comments, innuendo, gestures, threats or physical contact. Anyone engaging in these types of behavior could be charged with harassment under the policies of the institution in which they are working or assault under prevailing laws of their community.

---

[1] This term was coined by Tom Humphries and refers to the notion that one is superior based on one's ability to hear or behave in the manner of one who hears (Zak's Politically Incorrect Glossary, submitted by James Womack, 14 Sept 1994).

2.0   Guard Client's Personal Dignity and Right to Self-Determination/Empowerment

2.1   Be aware of any personal bias or reactions (positive or negative) which might threaten the quality of service provided.

When relating to others, professionals are expected to actively respect the individual uniqueness of each person with whom they work. This is possible only if each practitioner is able to ensure her/his neutrality within professional interactions.

While we are expected to maintain respect toward all, we enter professional settings as human beings with our own unique personal history, including conscious and unconscious prejudices. It is critical that we constantly monitor our actions, reactions, and attitudes, searching for any personal bias that might compromise our ethical integrity and thereby failing to respect the personal choices and rights of clients/students to chart their own destiny.

2.0   Guard Client's Personal Dignity and Right to Self-Determination/Empowerment

---

APPLYING THE STANDARDS
Peter Pan is an ASL/English interpreter. He is also a devout member of a particular religious group. He wears a medallion around his neck that is a common symbol of his religious group. When called to interpret in a professional setting, he is mindful to place his medallion inside of his shirt — just in case it might be offensive to someone present at the interpreted event. **REFLECTING ON PAN'S SITUATION:** Pan is being sensitive to the multi-religious fabric of his community. His choice is a good one Pan also needs to be aware of the topics and clients he may encounter in various interpreting assignments. Because he has strong religious convictions, he needs to be aware of what topics may affect his ability to serve his client appropriately. No one can or should abandon their personal beliefs and convictions. However, professionals learn how to balance professional decisions with personal beliefs.

As noted in the following example, if we feel our neutrality may be compromised, we may need to ask a colleague to reflect on and/or monitor our work. It may be necessary, for example, for a teacher to ask another faculty member to check their scoring of a particular student's assignments to ensure fairness in marking. An interpreter may ask a colleague to observe their work or review a videotape of their work to check for accuracy and absence of impropriety. This

2.0   Guard Client's Personal Dignity and Right to Self-Determination/Empowerment

type of diligence helps each of us maintain our ethical integrity as concerned professionals.

APPLYING THE STANDARDS

Phrootloop teaches full time in a Sign Language interpreting program. She does her best to treat all students equally and to maintain visual neutrality in her relationships with students. One student this semester is driving her crazy! The student is resistant and confrontational at every level. She looks bored and her boredom is reflected in her body language — loud and clear. Phrootloop has spoken with the student and attempted to identify underlying problems but to no avail. Phrootloop holds her own throughout the semester but is quite relieved when final exams are over, knowing she will not have to deal with this irritating student any longer.

REFLECTING ON PRHOOTLOOP'S SITUATION: This is a difficult situation. Most interpreting programs have limited faculty members, making it impossible to simply transfer a student from one section of a class to another. Phrootloop would be wise to build some additional safeguards to protect herself and the student. For example, when exams come around, Phrootloop should ask a colleague to mark this student's tapes/papers — just to be sure no negative bias is influencing the marks she assigns to the work.

2.0   Guard Client's Personal Dignity and Right to Self-Determination/Empowerment

2.2   In working relationships maintain the confidentiality of clients and/or students unless there is a legal mandate to report.[2]

INTERPRETERS — working relationships. The interpreting relationship and all related information must be kept confidential. This means that everything an individual sees, hears, or learns within the interpreted event is

---

[2] The safety and welfare of vulnerable individuals supersedes professional requirements of confidentiality. In most states/ provinces, professionals are legally required to inform responsible authorities when a client and/or student discloses that s/he:

(a) Is the perpetrator or victim of sexual abuse;

(b) Indicates clear and imminent danger to him/herself or others (e.g. threats of suicide or intent to harm).

In limited situations, a professional may also be required to take reasonable personal action in order to reduce harm or danger to others while maintaining personal safety. In some cases, confidential consultation with other professionals is appropriate.

In most situations involving an ASL/English interpreter, other professionals are present who are required to report such information (doctors, social workers, therapists, etc). Thus interpreters are rarely the source of such a report.

2.0   Guard Client's Personal Dignity and Right to Self-Determination/Empowerment

confidential — including anything that comes as a result of being in a place where s/he is providing interpreting services.

In cases where an interpreter works as a member of a professional team, others on the team are also bound by confidentiality. It is also understood that the goal of such consultations is to maximize service delivery to the client(s).

When working with a team interpreter, orienting a substitute interpreter or when leaving an ongoing interpreting job, any history is pertinent to the success of the interpretation. Therefore, it is appropriate for the interpreters involved to consult with each other regarding specialized or technical vocabulary, and the client's communication preferences and idiosyncrasies. It is understood that the purpose of such consultations is to maximize the ability of the interpreters to provide quality service to the client(s) and not to gossip or engage in gripe sessions.

TEACHERS — working relationships: The relationship of teachers with students is less likely to give rise to issues of confidentiality. However there are several areas that are impacted by this principle:

2.0   Guard Client's Personal Dignity and Right to Self-Determination/Empowerment

- Teachers should never discuss one student with another student.

- If student information is routinely shared with other faculty or instructional team members, students should be informed of this at the beginning of each semester/quarter.

- When speaking with other members of the instructional team, personal information about a student should be guarded as much as possible. A teacher should only discuss the information required to address a student's educational performance.

- Student documents, samples of student work (written or taped) should not be used outside of the classroom setting without the written permission of the student.

Because there are some settings within which we can share or discuss some client/student information, it is easy to become careless about the content of our comments. In an effort to safeguard creeping insensitivity to violations of confidentiality, professionals are individually responsible for setting a norm of confidentiality in private and group interactions. When one of our colleagues makes a comment that is in violation of this ethical principle, whether inadvertent or deliberate, casual or preplanned, it is incumbent on each of us to respond in a way that reminds our colleague of the requirement for confidentiality.

2.0   Guard Client's Personal Dignity and Right to Self-Determination/Empowerment

---

APPLYING THE STANDARDS

Central College employs a large number of contract interpreters to serve the 60-plus Deaf students who take classes there. One day Drum, Zenith, Daffodil, and Mustang (all of whom work as interpreters at Central) are eating lunch in the cafeteria. When Ethellene, another interpreter on campus, enteres the room, she stopped by their table and said, "My Gosh! Is Cinnamon *ever* gonna get her act together? *Once again* she was supposed to make a class presentation today and she was absolutely loony tunes! How am I supposed to do a decent job interpreting?" As soon as the words were out of her mouth, she rushed on to the serving line.

Drum and Daffodil look at each other in amusement. But Zenith had a look of consternation on her face. She said to the others, "Did I just hear what I think I heard? Did Ethellene just violate a student's confidentiality?" The others laughed and said, "Oh no — Ethellene always 'runs off at the mouth' like that."

Zenith was still concerned. She now knew something about a student that she had not known before. The information had come from someone who could *only* have learned that information in a confidential relationship with the student. Further, the information might influence Zenith's perception of that student in the future.

REFLECTING ON ZENITH'S SITUATION: Unfortunately, this type of event happens more frequently than we would like to admit. It is more likely to happen where a group of professionals share a common work site — and sometimes the same clients/students — or where two practitioners work closely together, frequently referring work to one another.

It is almost as if the professional relationship and frequent contact results in a relaxing of ethical vigilance. This is *not* acceptable! When professionals get together, they need to be extra diligent to ensure that their conversation is free from any content that could violate the privacy rights of clients/students.

2.0   Guard Client's Personal Dignity and Right to Self-Determination/Empowerment

---

APPLYING THE STANDARDS

Cocktail teaches at State University. One day two of her friends make a presentation to her class. Afterward they went out for coffee and during the conversation, someone mentioned how sickly one of the students in class looked.

Cocktail responds, "Well, I think she looks great considering that she is HIV positive and has lost her husband and their oldest child to AIDS over the last six months."

"Oh, how awful for her," exclaims one of Cocktail 's friends, as the other nods her head in agreement. Cocktail continues, filling her friends in on all the details.

REFLECTING ON COCKTAIL'S SITUATION: Teachers, like all other professionals, have access to confidential information about students that must be guarded. Cocktail 's revelation is an unethical violation of the trust placed in her by this student, even if she received the information from some source other than the student herself.

2.3   Clients must be informed of any special conditions prior to entering an interpreting relationship, including a duty to report.

There are some places where the principle of confidentiality does not apply. For example, an interpreter can be subpoenaed to testify about the content of an interpreted police interrogation or an interview conducted by a social

2.0   Guard Client's Personal Dignity and Right to Self-Determination/Empowerment

worker. Members of the Deaf community generally assume that any information exchange to which an interpreter is privy is confidential. Therefore the interpreter is obligated to clarify issues of her/his role, responsibility, use of video recording, and lack of confidentiality with the Deaf client(s) before starting to interpret in these types of settings.

APPLYING THE STANDARDS

Armadillo's parents are Deaf so she has interacted with members of the Deaf community in a variety of settings for most of her life. She works as an interpreter primarily in legal settings.

Any time Armadillo is called to the police station to interpret for an arrest or interrogation, she knows that the Deaf individual involved is usually *very* relieved to see someone they know and with whom they can communicate.

Armadillo also knows that in their excitement at seeing her enter the room, the Deaf individual is also often tempted to launch into a narrative about what happened and why s/he is at the police station.

Because of this, Armadillo *always* diverts her eyes and begins signing, "Wait — you need to know that if you tell me anything here, I can be forced to go to court and tell the judge what you said." Armadillo then makes

2.0   Guard Client's Personal Dignity and Right to Self-Determination/Empowerment

eye contact with the Deaf individual to be sure s/he understands that the rules for confidentiality here are different from other places.

REFLECTING ON ARMADILLO'S SITUATION: There are pros and cons to Armadillo's choice here. She is doing a good job of alerting the Deaf client about a variation in the "normal" rule of confidentiality.

At the same time, she may be setting up a type of "alarm" or "alert" to the Deaf individual that undermines the goal of the police officer. Further, she will have to be very careful about the nonverbal (facial) affect that accompanies her initial comment. Some facial behaviors might make the Deaf client think that Armadillo has already decided s/he did something wrong. Other facial behaviors, particularly if accompanied by certain physical gestures, may look like a reprimand and/or condescension toward the Deaf individual. Finally, the police officer may find the communication suspect — as if the interpreter is in collusion with the Deaf individual.

If an interpreter has limitations of time or availability, or if interpreted sessions are to be observed by a mentor or interpreting student, both Deaf and hearing clients must be contacted to give consent in advance of the interpreted event.

2.0   Guard Client's Personal Dignity and Right to Self-Determination/Empowerment

---

APPLYING THE STANDARDS

Nutmeg works as a self employed Sign Language interpreter. In addition, she mentors graduating interpreting students from the local college. The student will accompany her to a medical appointment today.

When this appointment was set up two weeks ago, Nutmeg informed the doctor's appointment nurse, that she would be working with an interpreting intern and asking if the doctor would have any objection. She deliberately chose the term "intern" because that is the term familiar to people in medical settings. The nurse checked with the doctor and confirmed that it would be fine to bring the intern. Nutmeg then called the Deaf client. She explained who the student was, the fact that she would be observing and — if the Deaf client approved — interpreting for the x-rays that were to be taken. Nutmeg reassured the client that she would be right by her side so no communication would be lost, but restated that if the client had any reservations, Nutmeg would not bring the student with her. The Deaf client agreed to have the student present.

REFLECTING ON NUTMEG'S SITUATION: Nutmeg is modeling appropriate behavior in this situation. She is fairly certain about what will happen at the appointment and believes it to be a safe place for a student to accompany her. In addition, had either party shown hesitation or uncertainty, Nutmeg would have withdrawn her request.

Further, Nutmeg is sensitive to the fact that the Deaf client may change her mind on the day of the appointment, particularly if she is feeling nervous or uneasy. She has alerted the interpreting student and prepared her for the possibility of being told to wait in the lobby at the last minute if necessary.

2.0   Guard Client's Personal Dignity and Right to Self-Determination/Empowerment

The cultural norms and taboos of Deaf culture sometimes require Sign Language professionals to make decisions counter to the norms and expectations of mainstream culture. For example, courtroom events are considered public — meaning anyone can drop in on a trial or legal hearing and observe what is going on there. However, given the size of the Deaf community and the principle of guarding the rights and personal dignity of each client, it is not appropriate for the interpreter to invite a mentor or interpreting students to these types of "public" settings. To do so would result in breaking confidentiality and damaging one's professional relationships with the community.

APPLYING THE STANDARDS

Douglas College is located next door to the Provincial Law Courts building in New Westminster, British Columbia. There are times when a trial is being held at the Law Courts involving Deaf litigants, witnesses, victims, etc. Some of these are high profile cases so there are also times when the courtroom is filled with a variety of Deaf observers.

2.0   Guard Client's Personal Dignity and Right to Self-Determination/Empowerment

While trials are in session, the tables at the college cafeteria often fill up with Deaf individuals because the prices are the least expensive in the area. In spite of the public nature of such events, the faculty in the interpreting program does not make arrangements for their student to go to court to observe legal interpreters at work — in spite of the fact that such an experience would be extremely valuable to the students.

However, Douglas College students have attended two court sessions. The first was a Supreme Court hearing and the second was a hearing in which the judge was to determine whether or not a request for a class action suit would be approved. In both cases, the Deaf community appealed for as many people as possible to attend in order to impress the judges with the support of members of the community. In addition, no Deaf witnesses were testifying at either hearing, thus in no way could the privacy of any of the litigants be compromised.

2.4   Teaching professionals are expected to create a safe environment within which students are respected and their welfare is promoted.

Like all professionals, teachers are characterized by filling a role of power and authority. Teachers evaluate student performance and determine if a student will pass or fail a class. Further, ASL and interpreting students are required to

2.0   Guard Client's Personal Dignity and Right to Self-Determination/Empowerment

become quite vulnerable as they demonstrate evolving skills in front of classmates. It is easy for individual students to feel fearful, uncomfortable, and unsafe in such a setting.

APPLYING THE STANDARDS

Fansie Fingers is a student at State University. She is taking ASL in preparation for admittance to the interpreting program. She entered the semester excited about her courses.

However, her ASL classes have been painful. It is clear that the teacher favors two students in the class, engaging them in conversation frequently and praising their signing skills. When Fansie signs, the teacher rolls her eyes and lets out a big breath before telling her she isn't making sense and turning away.

It is now near the end of the semester and Fansie is thinking about dropping out of school. She feels stupid, inept, and has begun to lose her confidence.

REFLECTING ON FANSIE'S SITUATION: Fansie's ASL instructor is not conducting herself in a professional manner. All students should feel valued and respected. They should be treated equally by their teachers, regardless of the diversity in their learning curve.

2.0   Guard Client's Personal Dignity and Right to Self-Determination/Empowerment

A safe learning environment is characterized by:

❖ Information presented in ways that meet the students' individual learning styles;

❖ Teachers who listen to their students and make modifications to the teaching plan as needed;

❖ A supportive environment in which — because of encouragement, not ridicule — students can demonstrate what they are learning and the skills they are developing;

❖ Regular feedback is given in an honest and encouraging manner on both written and skills performances;

❖ Confirmation that the instructor believes in the student's ability to learn, that learning is a process and that the process of learning requires one to try new things and risk mistakes;

❖ Reminders that the classroom is the best place to take risks;

❖ An instructor who takes action to resolve any negative or unhealthy group dynamics or harassment that might emerge in a class.

3.0   Assume Responsibility for Consumer Satisfaction and Quality of Service

3.1   Confirm that client/students are satisfied with the overall quality of interpretation/instruction.

An ethical professional takes personal responsibility for the quality of the work provided. S/he accepts the consequences of inappropriate decisions made and actions taken. While it is difficult to accept criticism of our behavior, it is the hallmark of an ethical and emotionally healthy individual.

Professionals are responsible for seeking confirmation that their client's/student's needs are being met. In order to do this, one must seek out and embrace ongoing critique of their professional decisions and quality of service. This feedback is sometimes overtly expressed by a client/student when, for example, they are dissatisfied with the service provided. Feedback is often subtle, found in a facial expression or a hesitation on the part of the client/student in question. For that reason, professional accountability requires open acceptance and reflective evaluation of feedback, or honest critique. The professional will not allow sensitivity to lead to frustration or rejection of a helpful suggestion. Every part of feedback should be utilized as a stepping stone to achievement.

3.0   Assume Responsibility for Consumer Satisfaction and Quality of Service

---

APPLYING THE STANDARDS
KarmelKorn is a Sign Language interpreter, having graduated from an interpreting program ten years ago. She has contracts at two colleges where she interprets a total of 25 hours per week. In addition, she does some freelance work in medical and employment settings.

After a recent team interpreting experience, KarmelKorn's partner asked for time to debrief after the appointment. During that time, her partner asked KarmelKorn about several choices she had made and suggested some other options. Her partner also suggested that KarmelKorn consider the visual background provided by the pale pink blouse, given that she had a fair complexion.

KarmelKorn was livid! Her interpretation and choice of clothing had never been questioned before. She stomped out of the debriefing session, determined never to work with that partner again.

REFLECTING ON KARMELKORN'S SITUATION:
KarmelKorn — and her clients — would be better served if she could engage in the debriefing discussion without becoming defensive. Reflective, evaluative discussion of one's work is imperative if a practitioner is to ensure the best service possible to one's clients/students. Failing to engage in this type of evaluation may lead to poor quality of service. |

3.0   Assume Responsibility for Consumer Satisfaction and Quality of Service

---

APPLYING THE STANDARDS

After a recent interpreting appointment, Donna and Darnell Deaf asked Beammer if he would go for coffee with them. He agreed but as they sit down in the restaurant, Donna and Darnell begin to talk about how Beammer needs to work on his signing and interpreting skills. Some of the signs used, they explain, are offensive and inappropriate for the place where the interpreting was taking place. In addition, they are concerned with some of the facial expressions he uses and the visibility of his tongue as he signs.

Beammer is caught off guard and is a bit defensive initially. Then he remembers that critique/feedback is a gift of encouragement and direction in the Deaf community. Until now, he has assumed his interpreting was acceptable but here are two individuals who care enough to give him some difficult but much needed feedback. He listens carefully, tries to duplicate the signs and facial features being modeled, and thanks Darnell and Donna when they leave the restaurant.

REFLECTING ON BEAMMER'S SITUATION: Members of the hearing community often confuse feedback with criticism. Beammer is correct in realizing that feedback is offered from members of the Deaf community as a signal that they value a person. If they don't believe an individual has potential as an interpreter or if a person displays a culturally inappropriate attitude, Deaf community members won't give that person direct feedback.

3.0   Assume Responsibility for Consumer Satisfaction and Quality of Service

In 1998, it was alleged that President Bill Clinton had a sexual affair with a White House intern half his age. His first reaction was anger and denial. When the truth finally came out months later, Mr. Clinton had difficulty accepting responsibility for his unprofessional and unethical acts, including the fact that he had lied and used legal technicalities to avoid responsibility. In response to this situation, Senator Kerry (Dem. Nebraska) made the following statement on television:

> I do not believe public leaders can condone the parsing of words into pieces so small that they no longer convey plain meaning. The coinage of democracy is language and I believe that when we distort the meaning of words we devalue the currency by which the commerce of democracy is conducted. Legal technicality is not an adequate standard of truth ... (Nightline, September 3, 1998, ABC Television: New York City).

Unfortunately, Mr. Clinton's reaction was not unique. All of us are in danger of sliding into a slippery ethical morass unless we habitually accept responsibility for our actions and decisions. Beware if you find yourself reacting to critique and feedback with anger, defensiveness, "parsing words" and reference to technicalities to justify your behavior.

3.0   Assume Responsibility for Consumer Satisfaction and Quality of Service

3.2   Remove yourself from a setting as soon as you realize an inability to meet the interpreting needs of a client.

There is no shame in declaring oneself unqualified to provide service for a particular individual or in a particular setting. As a matter of fact, it is unethical to remain in such a situation. An interpreter may remove her/himself because s/he lacks the requisite knowledge or skill required. In the same way a Judge may recuse her/himself from presiding over a particular case, an interpreter may remove her/himself because of a personal limitation, conflict with material being presented, or for any number of reasons. For example, an experienced interpreter may be highly qualified to work in court and various legal settings. However, s/he may not be qualified to interpret in medical settings – either because s/he is unfamiliar with medical terminology and protocol or because s/he faints at the sight of blood or the smells common to hospitals. An interpreter may go into a setting where s/he normally has the requisite knowledge and skill but encounters a client she is not able to understand.

3.0   Assume Responsibility for Consumer Satisfaction and Quality of Service

---

APPLYING THE STANDARDS

Egret is a freelance interpreter and has been working in the local community for 20 years. He interprets in a number of settings, including medical, mental health and legal. In addition, Egret teaches some courses in the local interpreting program.

The Deaf community has been all abuzz about an impending trial in which a member of the Deaf community has been charged with sexual misconduct toward minor Deaf children. Since it is a public setting, a number of Deaf individuals plan to attend the proceedings.

The court contacted Egret and asked him to be one of the members of the interpreting team for this trial. Egret asked the court coordinator for a list of potential Deaf witnesses to determine if he were comfortable interpreting for them. He noted the name of one individual with whom he has had some personal conflict. He contacted the court coordinator, explained that he knew this individual and suspected s/he would not feel comfortable with Egret as an interpreter. He suggested that the coordinator check with the individual to determine her/his level of comfort. If the witness did not want Egret as an interpreter, Egret offered to step aside or to be replaced by another interpreter for this one witness.

REFLECTING ON EGRET'S SITUATION: Egret is diligent in ascertaining his ability to provide quality service in this setting. In addition to identifying those for whom he will be providing interpretation, he should also familiarize himself with what charges have been laid in order to confirm that he is able to deal with that topic area.

3.0   Assume Responsibility for Consumer Satisfaction and Quality of Service

While the experienced practitioner will try a variety of strategies in an effort to communicate with the client, once s/he determines that communication is not successful because her/his skills are not adequate for this particular client, participants should be tactfully informed and the interpreter should withdraw service. This needs to be done in a manner sensitive to the dynamics between the individuals involved and the vulnerability of clients.

It is unethical for an interpreter to initiate or continue a professional relationship after realizing that s/he is unable to meet the interpreting needs of a client. In such instances, a recommendation may be made to secure the services of a Deaf (relay) interpreter,[3] or referral may be made to another, more appropriate interpreter. If the client declines the suggested referral, the professional is not obligated to continue the interpreting relationship.

---

[3] A Deaf Interpreter (DI) is an individual who is audiologically and culturally Deaf, preferably with training in interpretation. The DI interprets between the hearing ASL/English interpreter and the Deaf client(s), while the hearing ASL/English interpreter interprets between the DI and the non-deaf client. The use of Deaf Interpreters is strongly encouraged to ensure consumer satisfaction and quality assurance.

3.0   Assume Responsibility for Consumer Satisfaction and Quality of Service

---

APPLYING THE STANDARDS

Whiz graduated from the interpreting program 18-months ago. She has been working in the elementary school since graduation, primarily with kindergarten and first grade Deaf and hard-of-hearing children.

When one of the children is hurt on the playground, Whiz accompanies the child and the school nurse to the hospital to interpret. She is aware of the fact that she is having difficulty understanding the child — who seems to be "slurring" his signs. She also struggles to interpret the questions posed by the emergency room doctor. The thought crossed her mind to call a more experienced interpreter, but it quickly flits away.

The child's parents arrive and after consulting with the doctor, they authorize emergency surgery. Whiz stays, waiting with the parents through the surgery, going into the recovery room to interpret for the child and then accompanies him back to his hospital room.

Whiz remains a bit torn — thrilled with the opportunity to support the child and his family, excited about the chance to do some medical interpreting — but concerned because she knows information is getting lost and skewed at points. She decides not to worry about it, assuming that if there are any serious concerns, the parents will say something.

REFLECTING ON WHIZ'S SITUATION: At the moment the decision was made to transport this child to the hospital, an interpreter who was qualified to work in medical settings should have been called. By deciding to stay in a setting for which she was unqualified — especially when she knew information was being lost and/or misunderstood — Whiz violated her ethical guidelines.

Whiz should have told the doctors about the "slurred" signing since it could be of medical significance. Further, Whiz should have informed the medical personnel and parents at each point where she noted miscommunication happening, reminding them that she is not qualified to do this type of interpreting.

4.0   Relate Effectively Within the System(s) Involved

We do not work in a vacuum. In order to be most effective in our work, it is essential that professionals understand the system in which they are working.

4.1   Familiarize yourself with the policies, procedures, and lines of authority of systems within which you provide professional services.

It is critical that a practitioner understand who the key players are, what their roles and responsibilities are, and how they relate within the organizational structure. They should also familiarize themselves with the policies and procedures of the organization or institution.

APPLYING THE STANDARDS

Skateboard is one of six ASL teachers in an ASL Studies program. He has been a part of the faculty for seven years. A new program coordinator was hired six months ago and Skateboard is not happy with some of the changes being made. In frustration, he writes an angry letter to the President of the school, outlining his dissatisfaction.

4.0   Relate Effectively Within the System(s) Involved

The following week, Skateboard is summoned to the Dean's office for a meeting. As he enters, he sees that the new coordinator is also present in the meeting and that the Dean looks angry. The Dean shows Skateboard a copy of his letter and asks why he chose to go over her head to the President. He hesitates a bit and admits he really wasn't aware of the proper line of communication.

REFLECTING ON SKATEBOARD'S STUATION:
Skateboard may have had legitimate concerns, but his lack of sensitivity to the system in which he works may prevent his ability to ever get his grievances addressed. It is critical for practitioners to understand the policies, lines of authority, communication and procedures of various systems. Essential knowledge of this sort allows practitioners to access needed support and to make appropriate referrals.

4.2   Consult with other professionals when such consultation is needed to guarantee maximum service to clients/students.

It is common practice for professionals to consult with each other concerning complex or challenging cases. Thus, standard practice dictates that Sign Language professionals consult with each other when the goal is to ensure best practice is being provided.

4.0   Relate Effectively Within the System(s) Involved

In choosing consultants, teachers typically consult with other instructors in their school or college. Interpreters normally select another interpreter with equivalent or greater experience and skills base. When selecting a colleague with whom to talk, the practitioner should avoid placing the consultant in a conflict of interest situation.

Wherever possible, names and specific details that would reveal the identity of the client/student being discussed are protected. It is understood that where this is not possible, both professionals are bound by the ethical standard of confidentiality.

If a team of professionals meet on a regular basis to discuss the delivery of services to clients/students, they should inform those receiving their services that the norm of confidentiality applies to the team, not just to the individual practitioner. For example, in an interpreting program it is common to hold faculty meetings during which teachers discuss any student concerns they may have in order to address educational challenges uniformly. In order to be sure that students are aware that comments made to one teacher may be shared with other instructors in the program, a statement explaining that should be placed in the course outline or syllabus.

4.0   Relate Effectively Within the System(s) Involved

APPLYING THE STANDARDS

Jackpot has been interpreting between a Deaf individual and her/his therapist for four years. Due to a major change in her life, Jackpot will no longer be able to interpret for these clients. After speaking with both clients, she arranges for a new interpreter to take over this responsibility.

Jackpot meets with Venice, the new interpreter, to share critical information that will help Venice make as "seamless" a shift as possible. Jackpot explains that the client is in therapy because of multiple personality disorder (MPD). She identifies six personalities that have emerged over the past four years and discusses the sign name and communication style of each. Jackpot also describes some behaviors that precede a personality shift. She explains how this has helped alert her to an impending personality shift. Venice asks if Jackpot actually changes the pitch and tone of her spoken English to reflect each personality and Jackpot shares the techniques she has used.

When Venice asks about the therapist's goals in working with this client, Jackpot reminds her that she will meet with the therapist next week and suggests that she save her question for that meeting.

REFLECTING ON JACKPOT'S SITUATION: Jackpot has made appropriate and ethical decisions in the events described above. It would have been inappropriate to drop this challenging assignment in the lap of another interpreter without any preparation. At the same time, Jackpot has focused her comments on the task of interpretation, making no judgments on the client or therapist. Finally, Jackpot properly referred some questions to the therapist.

4.0   Relate Effectively Within the System(s) Involved

APPLYING THE STANDARDS

Vanna Bannanna is one of six ASL teachers in an ASL Studies program. The program coordinator and teachers meet every two weeks for a faculty meeting, discussing concerns about the program, equipment, students, etc. During the most recent meeting, Vanna shared her concerns about a particular student who has shown a pattern of arriving late to class, missing classes, falling asleep in class and generally showing decreased commitment to the program. As the instructors discuss this student, they agree that the coordinator should set up a meeting to discuss these concerns with the student.

At the meeting the student is very upset that the coordinator knows about her tardiness and absences. Later, she confronts Vanna angrily and accuses her of violating confidentiality. Vanna pulls out the course outline that was given to all students and discussed on the first day of class. She points out the following statement:

"Student progress, grades, attendance and participation in class will be discussed with program faculty during regular team meetings."

REFLECTING ON VANNA'S SITUATION: In this case Vanna has protected herself and the program from grievances that might arise from students. From the beginning she had alerted students to the rules governing the sharing of student information.

In addition, when students approach Vanna to tell her something that they want her to keep confidential, Vanna is prepared to say, "I will be glad to if I can, but if what you are going to tell me might affect your progression in the program, I will need to share it with the instructional team."

4.0   Relate Effectively Within the System(s) Involved

4.3   Maintain those records required by the institution and/or system, conscious of freedom of information legislation as well as legal liability (both individual and institutional).

When working in an institution or organization, professionals may be required to maintain certain records: names of clients being served, courses teaching/interpreting, attendance records, etc. Freedom of information legislation gives students/clients access to these records upon request. It is important that professionals exercise due care regarding the type and content of records kept.

Further, records can be subpoenaed by legal authorities in the event of civil or criminal action. This is true of documents maintained by professionals working freelance, on contract or as an employee of an agency and can include work schedules, notes, records of student progress, interview notes, test data, correspondence, audio/video recordings, notes made in preparation of an interpreting assignment and other documents. The law may also mandate that such documents be accessible to supervisors and others if the interpreting work is being done within an institution or agency. All practitioners should use discretion regarding how records are kept and the way information and individuals are represented therein.

4.0   Relate Effectively Within the System(s) Involved

APPLYING THE STANDARDS

Zebra is a certified interpreter, specializing in legal and mental health settings. She has contracted to serve as interpreter coordinator for a trial involving Deaf victims, witnesses, and defendants. The trial is scheduled to take place in six months

In the role of coordinator, Zebra selects teams of interpreters and notes the communication used by Deaf witnesses and defendants. She observes their language preferences, education and communication background, notes any unique communication tendencies and determines where/if the services of a Deaf interpreter will be required. Her notes include information such as: left handed signer, tendency to use contact signs, incomplete fingerspelled words, etc. Zebra uses these notes to prepare the interpreting teams prior to the appearance of each Deaf individual.

Two weeks before the trial is scheduled to begin, the prosecuting attorney calls Zebra to ask what written records related to the trial she may have. She describes the content of her notes and the prosecutor asks her to fax a copy to him because one of the defense attorneys has presented a discovery petition specifically requesting copies of notes in the possession of the interpreter coordinator. Zebra complies immediately.

REFLECTING ON ZEBRA'S SITUATION: This is common practice in the realm of our adversarial legal system. Because Zebra knew the system, she was cautious regarding the ways she described an individual's communication style, maintaining professional language and limiting recorded notes to the realm of her professional responsibility.

The same type of request could come to a teacher in response to a student appeal or a student's request for access to her/his records.

Appendix A

Guidelines for Ethical Decision-Making

I.   PROFESSIONAL COMPETENCE[1]

1.0   Be a Competent Practitioner

1.1   Possess bilingual and bicultural knowledge and skills that support appropriate community interaction, leading to formal or informal community endorsement.

1.2   Provide only those services for which you are qualified by training, experience and certification and which are culturally appropriate for you to provide.

1.3   Understand the constraints and responsibilities of professional roles from both mainstream (hearing) and minority (Deaf) cultural views.

1.4   Continue learning to ensure competent service and continued professional development.

---

[1] Principles regarding the knowledge and skills required in order for one to function in the role of a Sign Language professional.

II. PROFESSIONAL WORK ETHIC[2]

1.0 <u>Maintain Ethical Vigilance</u>: ideals of professional alertness to ethical impropriety.

    1.1 Regularly reflect on and think critically about professional decisions and actions in light of the Code of Ethics.

    1.2 Participate in collegial giving and receiving of constructive feedback with an eye to the healthy evolution of yourself and the profession.

    1.3 Take personal responsibility where inappropriate or unethical decisions and actions have been taken by yourself or your colleagues.

2.0 <u>Accept Professional Accountability</u>: standards of professional communication and self-representation.

    2.1 Claim or imply only those professional qualifications you actually possess.

    2.2 Information provided about a given situation or client, must:

        a) Be limited to your area of expertise;

        b) Conform to professional standards for confidentiality;

        c) Be accurate and unbiased; and

        d) Consist of factual, objective data.

---

[2] The level of industriousness, effort, energy and service required of a professional.

3.0   Present A Professional Image and
      Presence: suitability of dress, timeliness,
      and preparation for work.

   3.1   Comply with the norms for personal appearance
         when functioning in a professional role.

   3.2   Come to work prepared to provide the highest
         quality of professional service.

   3.3   Services rendered, including materials used, should
         reflect professional standards and quality.

   3.4   Take personal responsibility for quality of service
         provision.

4.0   Appropriate Fees for Service: norms in
      setting fees and providing pro bono
      service.

   4.1   Hold the needs of clients/consumers primary when
         making decisions regarding fees for service.

   4.2   Be aware of and sensitive to professional and
         cultural norms regarding fees for professional
         services.

III. Professional Relationships[3]

1.0 <u>Establish and maintain professional boundaries</u>: physical, social and psychological distance between the professional and her/his clients/students.

   1.1 Limit physical contact with your students/clients.

   1.2 Monitor your social interactions with students/clients.

   1.3 Maintain psychological separation between yourself and the students/clients with whom you work.

   1.4 Do not manipulate a work situation for personal benefit or potential harm to clients/students.

---

[3] Including a) conduct toward clients/students; b) behavior toward the institution within which one works; c) interactions with professional colleagues; and (d) interactions in the Deaf community.

2.0 Guard client's personal dignity and right to self-determination/empowerment: actions taken to support the interests and well being of individuals receiving professional services.

2.1   Be aware of any personal bias or reactions (positive or negative) that might threaten the quality of service provided.

2.2   In working relationships, maintain the confidentiality of clients/students unless there is a legal mandate to report.[4]

2.3   Clients must be informed of any special conditions prior to entering an interpreting relationship, including any duty to report.

---

[4] The safety and welfare of vulnerable individuals supersedes professional requirements of confidentiality. In most states/ provinces, professionals are legally required to inform responsible authorities when a client/student discloses that s/he:

(a) Is the perpetrator or victim of sexual abuse;

(b) Indicates clear and imminent danger to him/herself or others (e.g. threats of suicide or intent to harm).

In limited situations, a professional may also be required to take reasonable personal action in order to reduce harm or danger to others while maintaining personal safety. In some cases, confidential consultation with other professionals is appropriate.

In most situations involving an ASL/English interpreter, other professionals are present who are required to report such information (doctors, social workers, therapists, etc). Thus interpreters are rarely the source of such a report.

2.4   Teaching professionals are expected to create a safe environment within which students are respected and their welfare is promoted.

3.0   Assume responsibility for consumer satisfaction and quality of service: verification that service provided satisfied professional standards.

3.1   Confirm that client/students are satisfied with the overall quality of interpretation/ instruction.

3.2   Remove yourself from a setting as soon as you realize an inability to meet the interpreting needs of a client.

4.0   Relate effectively within the system(s) involved: maximize successful service delivery.

4.1   Familiarize yourself with the policies, procedures, and lines of authority of systems within which you provide professional services.

4.2   Consult with other professionals when such consultation is needed to guarantee maximum service to clients/students.

4.3   Maintain those records required by the institution and/or system, conscious of freedom of information legislation as well as legal liability (both individual and institutional).

Appendix B

Case Studies

WHAT WOULD YOU DO?

On the following pages, you will find a number of case studies for your consideration.[1] Using a separate journal to record your thoughts and reactions, reflect on each case study. Think through each situation carefully to determine what course of action you would take if you were the professional involved. Remember to apply the steps for decision-making studied in Chapter Two. In addition, consider the various ethical guidelines listed in Appendix A and expanded upon in Chapters Three, Four and Five.

Entries for each case study should address the following:

1. What facts/information do I have? Do I need more information before being able to move ahead?

2. What are the key ethical issues in the situation?

3. What are the applicable meta-ethical principles? (prioritize them if possible)

4. What options for action can you think of and what outcomes can you predict for each?

5. Identify your choice of action with rationale.

---

[1] Thanks to many students and colleagues who contributed ideas and actual case studies for inclusion in this text. This includes colleagues Byron Bridges, Debra Russell, Karen Malcolm, Cheryl Palmer, Sherry Burtnik, and Suzie Giroux.

CASE STUDIES FOR INTERPRETERS

<u>CASE STUDY: Interpreting #1.</u> You are working with Dragonfly, an interpreter in your community. You have done your prep work and both agreed that you would want feedback and notes and that your turns would be approximately 20-minutes in length. You have written encouraging and positive comments for your partner, along with a couple of linguistic questions. At the next spell off, Dragonfly takes over at 15-minutes and you note there is nothing written on the notepad explaining her early take over. After 20-minutes, you resume the working position, again having left a few notes for your partner. Once more, Dragonfly takes over at 15-minutes and leaves no notes on the notepad for you.

How do you feel? What are the ethical issues? What are your options? What will you do and why?

CASE STUDY: Interpreting #2. You are working with
Broadway, a talented new interpreter. You have completed
the prep session in which you have agreed to provide each
other with signed feeds if necessary. You are near the end of
1-1/2 hours. Thus far, each time you have needed a feed
Broadway has not given you one and each time you have
offered a feed, Broadway has chosen not to take it.

How do you feel? What are the ethical issues? What are
your options? What will you do and why?

CASE STUDY: Interpreting #3. You and your
colleague have never worked together before. You feel ready
for the day and have agreed to take 20-minute spells,
supporting each other with signed feeds as necessary. You
begin working and a few minutes later when you look to
your colleague for a feed, you are startled to see your
colleague take over. You wait patiently, thinking she will give
the work back to you, but she keeps interpreting. After 20-
minutes, you signal to her it is time to shift roles, but she
continues interpreting.

What are the ethical issues? What will you do and why?

CASE STUDY: Interpreting #4. You have been invited to work for a government agency that hires interpreters on an ongoing basis. The assignment is for a series of two day-long lectures, each month for six months. The agency hired one interpreter for this series last year and is proposing to hire you to work the series alone. You believe it is detrimental to your health to work these hours alone.

What are the ethical issues? What are your options? What will you do and why?

CASE STUDY: Interpreting #5. You work as an interpreter/classroom assistant for a deaf student in a classroom of 34 students. Part of your role is to interpret; part of your role is to work with all of the students in support of the teacher — grading papers, helping with learning activities, etc.

You have known the deaf student for several years and know his parents quite well. As a matter of fact, you socialize with the parents outside of work.

This student has begun displaying some behavioral problems at school, acting out, skipping class, and acting rude to you and to the teacher.

What are the ethical issues? What are your options? What will you do and why?

CASE STUDY: Interpreting #6. You are working in a classroom with a team interpreter. You are seated beside each other at the front of the class of about 40 students seated in theater arrangement. You are interpreting when your partner and a Deaf student begin a personal conversation in ASL.

What are the ethical issues? What are your options? What will you do and why?

CASE STUDY: Interpreting #7. You are interpreting with a ten-year-old who is the only Deaf student in the school district. The child is somewhat isolated and "clings" to you for communication, friendship and companionship. She wants to sit with you at lunch period and stand and talk with you during recess.

There is an educational planning meeting tonight. You will be attending, along with the teacher of the Deaf, the classroom teacher, the speech therapist, the school principal, and the Deaf student's parents. You are there to participate, not to interpret.

What are the ethical issues? What is your role? What types of questions can you respond to and what types of comments are you qualified to make? What are your options? What will you do and why?

CASE STUDY: Interpreting #8. While interpreting, your teammate's contact lens dislodges and she can't see. There are tears streaming down her face. She asks you to take over even though it is not yet time for your turn.

What are the ethical issues? What are your options? What will you do and why?

CASE STUDY: Interpreting #9. Local "tough kids" have been picking on a young Deaf student on the playground and on the way home each day. The mother of the Deaf child tells you about the situation and is obviously upset about it but she does not want you to do anything about it. She is afraid of reprisals against her child.

What are the ethical issues? What are your options? What will you do and why?

CASE STUDY: Interpreting #10. You are practicing for a holiday program in the school cafeteria with all grade 5 and 6 students. Some of the students have never seen a Sign Language interpreter before and they are staring at you as you interpret the instructions being given. One teacher says to the whole group, "Look at me ... not at the interpreter." Do you interpret the comment even though it is meant only for the hearing students?

What are the ethical issues? What are your options? What will you do and why?

CASE STUDY: Interpreting #11. You are working as an interpreter/classroom assistant in a kindergarten class. One day while sitting at a table with four hearing children and one five-year-old Deaf child, one child says to the Deaf student, "You're stupid! I hate you! You can't even hear!"

What are the ethical issues? Do you interpret the comment? What are your options? What will you do and why?

CASE STUDY: Interpreting #12. You and another interpreter have been booked to interpret a one-hour appointment between a Deaf social worker and the hearing parent of a Deaf child. You will both bill for the minimum two-hours.

Without telling you, your teammate calls the Deaf social worker in advance of the appointment explaining that he is really busy with another volunteer project and hopes the meeting finishes early if at all possible. She thanks your partner for the call and promises to do what she can to keep things on schedule.

You show up at the appointment, unaware of this earlier conversation. The two of you interpret the appointment that wraps up after only 35-minutes. The social worker thanks your interpreting partner and tells him he can go but that she would like you to stay and additional 30 to 45-minutes to interpret several telephone calls.

What are the ethical issues? What are your options? What will you do and why?

CASE STUDY: Interpreting #13. You have been interpreting for a particular student for three years. You are quite fond of him. He is a bright, talented kid but has some serious problem at home and is quite neglected. One day, the child protection services apprehend the boy, saying he is not safe at his home. The next day they contact you and ask if you would be willing to take the child into your home as a foster child — possibly for as long as one year.

What are the ethical issues? What are your options? What will you do and why?

CASE STUDY: Interpreting #14. You are interpreting for a six-year-old Deaf student. One day when she comes in from lunch, she wants to know what the kids mean when they put their middle finger up and what that word means.

What are the ethical issues? How far do you go in explaining that word? Or do you explain anything? What are your options? What will you do and why?

CASE STUDY: Interpreting #15. A kindergarten

teacher asks that a particular song or poem be signed in an English-like form to allow the whole class to sign and recite/sing the text. You have learned that music is not a part of the values of Deaf culture and that some Deaf people feel oppressed when forced to participate in auditory-based art forms like songs and poems.

What are the ethical issues? What are your options? What will you do and why?

CASE STUDY: Interpreting #16. You have very strong

beliefs against violence in any form. You are a member of several non-violence groups, march annually in anti-violence rallies, and do not allow any members of your family to watch TV programs that incorporate any form of violence — even stepping on spiders or using angry, heated verbal exchanges.

You are an interpreter for a grade-three child. One day when you go to work, you learn that a story that incorporates a number of violent interludes will be the focus of all class activities for the next three weeks.

What are the ethical issues? What are your options? What will you do and why?

CASE STUDY: Interpreting #17. You are 22-years old, working as an interpreter with Grade 12 Deaf students in a mainstreamed high school. One of the Deaf students for whom you interpret is quite mature for his age and has been flirting with you, making comments about your hair, body and clothes. His comments are "positive" but definitely in the category of "come-ons." The scary thing is that you are attracted to him.

What are the ethical issues? What are your options? What will you do and why?

CASE STUDY: Interpreting #18. You are interpreting for two ninth grade Deaf students. One day on your way to work, you stop by the corner store to get a latté. As you exit the store, you realize that several individuals you recognize as students — including one of the Deaf kids for whom you interpret — are making a drug purchase just outside of the store.

What are the ethical issues? What are your options? What will you do and why?

CASE STUDY: Interpreting #19. You have a contract
to interpret at a particular church each Sunday morning.
The church is made up of people of all ages, including
families with young children. You have a three-year old
daughter and always arrange for a sitter to take care of her
when you interpret at the church.

On this particular Sunday, your sitter cancels at the last
minute. You have called relatives and friends but no one is
able to take care of your daughter. Likewise, you have not
been able to find any other interpreter to cover the
assignment.

What are the ethical issues? What are your options? What
will you do and why?

CASE STUDY: Interpreting #20. You and a partner
will be interpreting for a staff meeting composed of 5 Deaf
and 4 hearing co-workers. As you discuss the assignment and
make teaming decisions, your partner asks you to do all of
the Sign to Voice work.

What are the ethical issues? What are your options? What
will you do and why?

CASE STUDY: Interpreting #21. You are working as an interpreter in the local high school. The parents of a grade 11 student approach you after school one day and ask you to interpret for the youth's driving lessons. They will be held one afternoon per week for four weeks plus four Saturday mornings beginning the following month. They explain that the driving school will not pay for interpreters and it is urgent for their child to get a driver's permit due to the illness of the father and physical disability of the mother.

What are the ethical issues? What are your options? What will you do and why?

CASE STUDY: Interpreting #22. You are single and work as an interpreter with grade six students. At a school function, you meet the single parent of the Deaf child for whom you interpret. You have an enjoyable chat and agree to meet for coffee later that week to get better acquainted. After two months, you have fallen for this parent and the feeling is mutual.

What are the ethical issues? What are your options? What will you do and why?

CASE STUDY: Interpreting #23. You interpret in a group rehabilitation setting for a Deaf individual who is disabled with cerebral palsy and is forced to use a wheelchair for mobility. He has a support worker with him who is responsible for helping him in and out of the bathroom, in and out of the van, and who assists with physical needs as necessary. The session you interpret for takes place in a gymnasium and involves a variety of physical activities.

Today, after about 30-minutes into the session, the Deaf client's support worker becomes ill and is forced to leave. The rehabilitation leader continues with the session, expecting you to take over the responsibilities of interpreting and physical support for the Deaf client.

What are the ethical issues? What are your options? What will you do and why?

CASE STUDY: Interpreting #24. You are working as an interpreter in the local high school. One day, the police make a locker search and find weapons in the locker of one of the Deaf students for whom you interpret. The principal calls you to the office and tells you to interpret for the police interrogation.

What are the ethical issues? What are your options? What will you do and why?

CASE STUDY: Interpreting #25. You have accepted a contract to interpret for a Deaf adult who is going through a six-week course designed to help participants secure employment. The classes have some lecture portions, but are mostly comprised of hands-on activities such as writing a resumé, making phone calls to set up mock job interviews, etc. For this reason, one interpreter has been employed to cover five class hours each day.

There are 50 students all together, one of whom is Deaf. The Deaf client has been a stay-at-home Mom for almost 20-years and has had very little contact with the hearing community. She is shy and uncertain of herself. From the very first day, she has "clung" to you during breaks, looking to you for emotional support and security.

What are the ethical issues? What are your options? What will you do and why?

CASE STUDY: Interpreting #26. You are a freelance interpreter whose daily schedule varies from day to day. Your "life line" is your cell phone. You use it to check your phone for messages, confirm appointments, negotiate requests for your services, etc.

You normally turn the cell phone off when you go into an interpreting appointment, but you left it on today because you are expecting a very important call regarding a job you are negotiating. Your phone rings right in the middle of the doctor's appointment you are interpreting.

What are the ethical issues? What are your options? What will you do and why?

CASE STUDY: Interpreting #27. You are on call to the local hospital for after hour's services. One early morning the phone rings. It is the hospital telling you there has been an auto accident and some of the injured are deaf. They need you right away. You jump up, throw on your clothes and hurry to the hospital. Once you arrive, you realize that the driver of the car is your boyfriend of three years. He is seriously injured.

What are the ethical issues? What are your options? What will you do and why?

CASE STUDY: Interpreting #28. You are interpreting at a Boy Scout meeting that involves Deaf and hearing youngsters. The Deaf father of a hearing Scout is engaged in a conversation with the Boy Scout leader after the meeting. They are discussing transportation to various events. The Deaf father has volunteered to drive the Scouts to and from a camp-out next weekend.

While interpreting this conversation, you realize that you know who this father is from some other interpreting experiences. You know that he is an alcoholic who has not been attending AA meetings — other AA members have made comment about his drinking again. You also recollect that this father has several drunk driving offenses in the past.

You are concerned about the safety of the Scouts in general and your nephew who will be attending the camp-out, in particular.

What are the ethical issues? What are your options? What will you do and why?

CASE STUDY: Interpreting #29. You are interpreting

for an elderly Deaf client who is scheduled to have major
surgery. You have interpreted an explanation about the
surgery by the doctor and instructions from the
anesthesiologist. You have made arrangements to scrub,
dress in greens and to go into surgery with the very nervous
client until she falls asleep. Everything has gone smoothly. At
the agreed upon time, you report to recovery so you can be
present as she begins to come out from under the drugs.
However, the head nurse in recovery refuses you
admittance. He won't even speak to you to let you explain
the circumstances.

What are the ethical issues? What are your options? What
will you do and why?

CASE STUDY: Interpreting #30. You have been

asked by a Deaf friend to interpret for a multi-level
marketing meeting. He is not able to pay you for your
services, but has offered to pay you by putting your name at
the top of the "list." This means that he will get ten of his
friends — probably all Deaf — to sign up and pay money. He
will place their names under yours, which means that you
are guaranteed a check of $500 within thirty-days.

What are the ethical issues? What are your options? What
will you do and why?

<u>CASE STUDY: Interpreting #31.</u> You interpret for a client at a rehabilitation facility for sexual offenders. All of the men in the group you interpret for are convicted rapists. Today during a break, you are outside chatting with the Deaf client who mentions the name of an interpreter you know. She has just moved to town, knows only a few members of the Deaf or interpreting community, and seems a bit young and naive.

The client describes how he met her, how attractive she is physically and the fact that he has made arrangements to meet her at a pub tonight. He indicates that he plans to have his way with her one way or another. You feel he is dangerous and his comments are threatening.

What are the ethical issues? What are your options? What will you do and why?

CASE STUDY: Interpreting #32. You are interpreting a series of parenting classes with a partner. The instructor and participants attending the class are dressed casually; the participants are primarily unemployed and/or on welfare and cannot afford to dress more formally than they do. Your teammate consistently over-dresses — hose, heels, and upscale business clothes. You believe your partner's choices are making the participants uncomfortable.

What are the ethical issues? What are your options? What will you do and why?

CASE STUDY: Interpreting #33. You interpret for a 13-year old Deaf student at school. You suspect that the boy's father is physically abusive. You have observed black eyes, large bruises, and broken fingers. John's behavior when you ask about the injuries and the look in his eyes when his father is present adds to your suspicions. The student is trying out for the school track team. As he is waiting for his turn to run, he mentions that if he doesn't make the team his father has told him he will break his toes.

What are the ethical issues? What are your options? What will you do and why?

CASE STUDY: Interpreting #34. You are a long-time interpreter and member of the Deaf community. You have interpreted in medical, mental health, psychiatric and drug rehabilitation settings.

You are called to interpret at the emergency room of the hospital. The hospital staff complains that this person is abusing the privileges since this is his 14th ambulance ride and admittance to the emergency room in the past three weeks with the same symptoms.

When the nurses try to get information from the patient, his responses are inappropriate. His eye behaviors seem unfocused and he is somewhat combative. You begin to suspect that there may be some psychological or drug basis to the behaviors you are seeing but none of the nursing staff seem to notice.

What are the ethical issues? What are your options? What will you do and why?

CASE STUDY: Interpreting #35.

You are an interpreter and a part-time instructor in the interpreter training program in the local college. You go to a large Deaf community social event where alcohol is served. You are there on your own time — not because you are a teacher or interpreter and not because you required some of your students to attend. However, you are aware of the fact that some interpreting students are present at the event.

These are your friends. It has been a long, hard month and you would really like to have a few drinks and let your hair down.

What are the ethical issues? What are your options? What will you do and why?

CASE STUDY: Interpreting #36.

You are team interpreting an event. You notice that your partner is nervous and that she intersperses the question "Do you understand?" every few phrases while interpreting. You are uncomfortable, sensing that it is coming from her lack of confidence but feeling that it is demeaning to the Deaf client.

What are the ethical issues? What are your options? What will you do and why?

CASE STUDY: Interpreting #37. Last week you
interpreted in a hospital Emergency Room for a Deaf
woman who had been severely beaten by her husband. You
note that the woman is a recent immigrant to this country
and not familiar with our social or legal system. In addition,
she has no written English skills and her signed
communication is somewhat limited. Her husband is not an
immigrant and has been a long-time member of the local
Deaf community.

The doctor expresses concern about the abuse but notes that
she is an adult. Unless she decides to file charges or to leave
her abuser, nothing can be done. Predictably, one-week later
you are called to the hospital and find yourself interpreting
for the same battered woman again.

What are the ethical issues? What are your options? What
will you do and why?

CASE STUDY: Interpreting #38. You have been interpreting for a particular client in the same setting for three years. The Deaf client is always bragging on you and saying what a great interpreter you are. You know the client tells other members of the Deaf community that you interpreter for him and that you are one of the best interpreters he has ever worked with. One day after an appointment, the client hands you a box in a shopping bag and says it is a gift — nothing fancy ... just an expression of appreciation for the wonderful quality of service over the past three years. He insists that you not open it until you get home. When you get home, you find an expensive leather jacket.

What are the ethical issues? What are your options? What will you do and why?

CASE STUDY: Interpreting #39. You are on call to the local hospital for after hour's services. One early morning the hospital called telling you there has been an auto accident and they need you right away. When you get there, you find a very drunk driver who has been involved in a single-car accident. Once the deaf individual has received medical attention, the police want to take him to the station for a breath analysis and questioning. They ask you to accompany them and continue interpreting at the station.

What are the ethical issues? What are your options? What will you do and why?

CASE STUDY: Interpreting #40. You are interpreting a high school class with another interpreter. It is the first night of the course and you have never worked with this colleague before. Your partner takes the first turn. When your partner is working, she waves her hand or wiggles her foot to force the student to maintain constant eye contact with her. When you assume the working position, your partner continues this behavior if the student fails to look at you. You can see that the student is getting quite upset.

What are the ethical issues? What are your options? What will you do and why?

CASE STUDY: Interpreting #41. You are a fairly new interpreter, having graduated from an interpreting program a few months ago. You interpret at a church each Sunday. The congregation of approximately 70 people includes 4 Deaf adults and 5 Deaf children. You accepted this job because you are able to get the songs and sermon in advance and can make adequate preparation to do a satisfactory job. The minister is aware of the fact that you are fairly inexperienced and has been quite helpful in getting preparatory materials to you.

Today in the middle of the service the minister pauses and says, "I'd like to do something different. Forget my sermon. I'd like to ask the interpreter to teach us all the signs to the first song that was sung today. It's such a beautiful song. I'm sure many of you are curious not only of how to sign it but what each of the signs mean. I'm going to turn this over to the interpreter and let her teach us the song and discuss the various meanings of the signs."

What are the ethical issues? What are your options? What will you do and why?

CASE STUDY: Interpreting #42. You have been interpreting for less than one year. You have agreed to interpret a one-day workshop with a teammate who has about the same background you have. Neither of you knows much about computers — the topic of the workshop — but you have received a packet of information, class hand-outs, etc. You believe you are ready for the challenge.

You arrive at the workshop site about 20-minutes before it is to start. The leader approaches you apologetically and explains that she sent you all of the wrong materials. She hands you another packet and walks off. You realize the contents deal with complex, technical concepts related to various computer languages and programming. You are WAY over your head.

What are the ethical issues? What are your options? What will you do and why?

CASE STUDY: Interpreting #43. You interpret for a student in a college course. This is your first time to interpret for this student and for this instructor. The instructor gives students time during class to work on their assignments. The Deaf student isn't interested in using her/his time that way and tries to engage you in conversation every time this happens. You make your responses short and try to avoid visual contact with the student in hopes that s/he will focus on the assignment.

Tonight the instructor sees the two of you signing and reprimands you in front of the class, "Please stop chatting with my student. You are preventing her/him from doing their work!"

What are the ethical issues? What are your options? What will you do and why?

CASE STUDY: Interpreting #44. You interpret for a 15-year old student in a Catholic school. In the religion class they are discussing the stories about Jesus healing the deaf and blind. The deaf student for whom you interpret only became deaf three years earlier and has just come to terms with her own deafness.

What are the ethical issues? What are your options? Do you interpret the stories and discussion in some way to make deafness seem less negative? Or ... What will you do and why?

CASE STUDY: Interpreting #45. You have just gotten a job as an interpreter at the state/provincial school for the deaf that has a wonderful reputation as a bilingual-bicultural program. You enter the staff lounge the first day and are shocked to see six interpreters sitting among five Deaf and three hearing teachers — all of whom can sign — but the interpreters are all talking. They are making no effort to include Deaf teachers in their conversation — as if they weren't even there. You want to bond with these interpreters — they will be your colleagues — but you feel quite uncomfortable. You believe this behavior is disrespectful of the Deaf people in the room.

When one of the interpreters says something to you, you decide to sign your answer. After all, everyone can understand that language so why not use the most common language? The interpreter rolls his eyes and says, "We don't sign during lunch. This is our break and we have to take care of our arms! NOW, what did you say?"

What are the ethical issues? What are your options? What do you do and why?

CASE STUDY: Interpreting #46. You have been interpreting for more than twenty years, are nationally certified and are a valued member of the Deaf community. The state/provincial Office of Public Health has approached you and asked you to sit on the committee that regulates and oversees the administration of interpreting services for all medical settings. You chat with some Deaf friends and interpreting colleagues, all of whom encourage you to accept the appointment.

As you prepare to attend the first meeting, you discover that no Deaf or hard-of-hearing individuals serve on the committee. When you inquire as to why, you are told that the cost of interpreting services is prohibitive and there are no plans to change the composition of the committee.

What are the ethical issues? What are your options? What do you do and why?

CASE STUDY: Interpreting #47. You are interpreting for a meeting involving Deaf, Deaf-Blind, hard-of-hearing and non-deaf participants. The client you are working with is Deaf-Blind. During the break, your client asks you to go to the chairperson (also Deaf-Blind) and have her add an item to the agenda. "Oh, by the way," she adds, "would you grab me a cup of coffee on your way back? Thanks." You know you can accomplish these tasks more quickly than the client could do alone, yet you know she is capable of taking care of herself. Further, you need a break!

What are the ethical issues? What are your options? What do you do and why?

CASE STUDY: Interpreting #48. You have gone to a college class to substitute for the regular interpreter who has been injured in an auto accident earlier in the day. You have taken this assignment assuming you will be able to handle things.

When you arrive, you discover that the Deaf student is making a class presentation that is worth 60% of her grade. She has no notes or English text to help you with the spoken interpretation. To your dismay and embarrassment, you are not able to understand the student at all! You are totally unfamiliar with the content being discussed.

What are the ethical issues? What are your options? What do you do and why?

CASE STUDY: Interpreting #49. Your Deaf friend calls and invites you to a Tupperware party at her place. You are thrilled since you are anxious to see your friend's house and you'd like an opportunity to meet more of the Deaf community members. You arrive for the party and are introduced to the woman in charge of the party as the interpreter for the evening! You are shocked since she had not asked you to interpret. You came as a guest and among other things, you are wearing a polka-dot blouse.

What are the ethical issues? What are your options? What do you do and why?

CASE STUDY: Interpreting #50. You interpret for two Deaf girls in a Grade 7 class. One day after class, one of the girls approaches the male teacher to ask for extra help. You interpret her questions and his answers. At the end of the conversation, he says to the student, "I see you are becoming a little woman! I'm glad you are finally wearing a bra." As he speaks, he runs his hand across the student's back and tugs slightly on her bra strap. The comment and behavior takes you by surprise because it is so off topic and uncharacteristic.

What are the ethical issues? What are your options? What do you do and why?

CASE STUDY: Interpreting #51. You have just finished interpreting a public event. You feel like you did a fairly good job and comments of the Deaf audience indicate their satisfaction. As you leave another interpreter approaches you. He was in the audience and says quite bluntly that you did a very poor job, skewing the message and deleting many important concepts. He says, "You have no business doing something like this — you just have a long way to go." He abruptly leaves.

This individual has been an interpreter for many years although he has never received any formal training, is not a member of the interpreter organization and does not attend upgrading workshops.

What are the ethical issues? What are your options? What do you do and why?

CASE STUDY: Interpreting #52. You are interpreting

for a meeting between a grass roots Deaf individual and a government official. The Deaf individual is seeking a government grant under a special program for disabled entrepreneurs. The official continually refers to the Deaf individual as "hearing impaired" and once uses the term "deaf mute." You know these terms come from ignorance rather than an attempt to be offensive. You also know the Deaf client well enough to be concerned about what his reaction would be if those terms were interpreted.

What are the ethical issues? What are your options? What do you do and why?

CASE STUDY: Interpreting #53. You arrive at the

location for your next interpreting assignment — the personnel office of a large company. The Deaf individual applying for the job has not yet arrived but the woman in the personnel office insists that you come back to her office and wait there for the applicant to arrive. You are uncomfortable in doing that, but you aren't sure what else to do. In her office, she begins to quiz you about Deaf people in general and this applicant (who happens to be a friend of yours) in particular. You keep hedging, suggesting that they wait until the applicant arrives. The personnel woman is quite persistent.

What are the ethical issues? What are your options? What do you do and why?

CASE STUDY: Interpreting #54.
You are interpreting for a swimming class of 8 and 9 year-old children. You are in the pool with the children, three of whom are deaf. One child continues to come up from under water at the end of each lap with a mouth full of water and spit it all over you. The instructor and the other Deaf children see what is happening. The instructor doesn't say anything.

What are the ethical issues? What are your options? What do you do and why?

CASE STUDY: Interpreting #55.
You are hired by two hearing individuals to interpret for them in a meeting with a Deaf co-worker. In the midst of the meeting, one of the hearing individuals says, "Let's take a break, OK?" He looks at you and says, "I need to speak confidentially with my partner. Don't interpret this please." He then turns and begins speaking in full voice with the second hearing person. Although a break has been called, the deaf client has not moved from his chair.

What are the ethical issues? What are your options? What do you do and why?

CASE STUDY: Interpreting #56. You are the staff interpreter in a large corporation that employs approximately 75 Deaf workers. You are called to the personnel office because one of the Deaf employees is filing a formal grievance against someone. When you get there you find that the grievance is being filed by an individual who has quite a reputation as a trouble maker. You know from socializing with the Deaf community that he is very unpopular because he is always making up stories and allegations against others. Further, the complaint is being filed against an outstanding employee and member of the Deaf community. You are quite sure something suspicious is going on here.

The personnel officer wants to set up a meeting immediately with the supervisor of the accused individual and a security officer so they can speak with the complainant. Following that, they will meet with the accused individual. They expect you to interpret for all of these meetings. You are aware of your bias and feel uncomfortable doing so.

What are the ethical issues? What are your options? What do you do and why?

CASE STUDY: Interpreting #57. You live in a small community and have been the only interpreter in town for 15 years. A Deaf woman with whom you have been friends for a number of years asks you to interpret for the upcoming birth of her first child.

You are uncomfortable with this situation. The father of her child is a former boyfriend of yours. You broke up three years previously and have avoided interpreting for him ever since.

What are the ethical issues? What are your options? What do you do and why?

CASE STUDY: Interpreting #59. You interpret in an educational setting with 20 students, 5 of whom are Deaf, a hearing teacher and a Deaf teaching assistant. The teacher has a habit of asking you questions concerning the progress of the Deaf students. You keep directing the questions towards the teaching assistant but it is clear the teacher still doesn't understand your role. Further, you feel she is not showing proper respect toward the Deaf teaching assistant.

What are the ethical issues? What are your options? What do you do and why?

CASE STUDY: Interpreting #59. You go to the police station to interpret for an appointment between a detective in the sex crimes division and a Deaf individual. The appointment was initiated by the Deaf individual so the police officer has no idea what the meeting is about. When the client arrives, you see it is a woman who uses ASL — someone you have never met before. As the appointment begins, the woman begins to describe an experience of being stalked and repeatedly raped. She is extremely emotional and her story is highly descriptive. When the officer asks the name of the perpetrator, the woman says, "It was Biel Llehctim." You stop cold. You have been dating Biel Llehctim for the past six months.

What are the ethical issues? What are your options? What do you do and why?

CASE STUDY: Interpreting #60. You are interpreting for a Cub Scout meeting where the boys are practicing tying various types of knots. One of the Deaf boys gets frustrated and starts saying, "This is stupid! I don't get it!" One of the leaders is circulating among the boys and you let him know of this child's frustration and need for assistance but he just walks on as if he doesn't hear you.

What are the ethical issues? What are your options? What do you do and why?

CASE STUDY: Interpreting #61. You first began
interpreting for a community theater troupe in a workshop
developing a script. Recently you began interpreting for the
rehearsals. Everybody is rather laid back and things are very
informal. One evening the director asks you to stay and
interpret for one of the Deaf actresses. After a very short
time, you realize that he is flirting suggestively with the Deaf
individual. She is only 15 years old and he is at least 30. The
young woman is quite flattered, but you have a sense that
this guy is trouble and knows quite well that he is taking
advantage of her innocence.

What are the ethical issues? What are your options? What
do you do and why?

CASE STUDY: Interpreting #62. You interpret for an
ongoing course one evening per week with another
interpreter. About mid-semester you are contacted and
asked to interpret for a very special community event. You
are flattered and excited about the opportunity. It conflicts
with this ongoing class but you know you can make
arrangements for a substitute. Unfortunately you discover
that your teammate is going out of town on that evening and
will also be sending in a substitute. If you accept the other
assignment, it will mean two substitutes in class who have
never worked with this client or in this class before.

What are the ethical issues? What are your options? What
do you do and why?

CASE STUDY: Interpreting #63. You and a teammate

are interpreting for a seminar. The Deaf client uses a contact variety, which you are trying to match, but your partner is using ASL with very little influence from English at all. At noon the client asks privately if you would do the afternoon session alone since he is having difficulty understanding the other interpreter.

What are the ethical issues? What are your options? What do you do and why?

CASE STUDY: Interpreting #64. An interpreter that

you know and respect has just obtained a very nice part-time job that pays quite well. You are happy for her — this will allow her to spend more time with her family and let her pursue freelance interpreting.

In another context, you learn a Deaf acquaintance had applied for a part-time job at the same company where your friend is now working. The Deaf acquaintance mentions that your friend interpreted for the job interview and that she is quite disappointed at not getting the job because the pay was quite comfortable.

Suddenly, alarm bells start to go off for you. You begin to wonder how your friend got the job ... heard about the job.

What are the ethical issues? What are your options? What do you do and why?

<u>CASE STUDY: Interpreting #65</u>. You graduated from an interpreting program last spring and have been hired to interpret in a local high school. You are keen on doing a good job. and actively seek feedback regarding your work — most of which is positive. All of the students are positive in regard to your work. In the beginning, all of the Deaf students have paid close attention to the interpretation. After about two months, one student gets a new boyfriend and starts spending most of the class time flirting with him rather than paying attention to class.

At midterm this student receives failing grades. She is very upset. She goes to the interpreter supervisor and says that while you are a really nice individual, your interpreting skill is quite limited. She blames her poor grades on your inadequate interpreting. The interpreting coordinator calls you in for a meeting.

What are the ethical issues? What are your options? What do you do and why?

CASE STUDY: Interpreting #66. You are employed to interpret for a GED class. The Deaf student is mono-lingual ASL and has very little confidence concerning school and interactions with hearing people. The teacher has never worked with a Deaf student or interpreter before. He orders the two of you to the back corner of the class. When you try to explain your needs he says, "You aren't a student in this class. If you can't do it my way then get out." You decide that for the time, you will try to fit in. He starts talking about the class and is rattling off information at the rate of a mile a minute. You raise your hand and ask him to repeat something. He says, "If you can't keep up this isn't the class for you," and goes right on talking.

What are the ethical issues? What are your options? What do you do and why?

CASE STUDY: Interpreting #67. You are interpreting for an auto mechanics class. All of the students and teachers are men — you are the only female in the whole building. The students make a point of using sexual innuendoes or sexist language. The instructor subtly encourages them and adds his comments as well. While students are working independently on projects, you stay close by but aren't needed to interpret. During these times, the teacher flirts, brushes past you in such a way as to "accidentally" touch your breasts or derrière.

What are the ethical issues? What are your options? What do you do and why?

CASE STUDY: Interpreting #68. You interpret for a

grade six child in a nearby elementary school. On Friday
evening, you and your date have made plans to meet some
friends at a restaurant for dinner. Much to your surprise, the
date of one of your friends is the classroom teacher with
whom you work on a daily basis. Over dinner the teacher
begins to ask you about the student, mentioning specifically
some behavioral problems he has. He is seeking your input
and advice.

What are the ethical issues? What are your options? What
do you do and why?

CASE STUDY: Interpreting #69. You work in a

Middle School with a teacher who expects you to discipline
the Deaf students in class. You have been hired as an
educational interpreter and have been told specifically that
you are not to take on any teacher responsibilities. When
you meet with the teacher to clarify your role and
responsibilities, he lets out a big sigh and says, "What a waste
of district money. That's ALL you do? Just interpret?
Sheesh!"

What are the ethical issues? What are your options? What
do you do and why?

CASE STUDY: Interpreting #70. You accompany a friend of yours (also an interpreter) to her family reunion. While there, your friend insists on introducing you to everybody by describing the fact that you are both interpreters. She goes on to explain that you work together, names the place where you work, the names of Deaf and hearing clients, and details about what has gone on during the interpreting assignment. You are very uncomfortable and keep trying to re-direct the conversation. The whole evening falls apart when an uncle of your friend says he knows the employees involved in the interpreting assignment — he works for the same company.

What are the ethical issues? What are your options? What do you do and why?

CASE STUDY: Interpreting #71. You have interpreted several counseling sessions between a therapist and a Deaf client. After the last session, the therapist asks you to stay. He begins to ask you how you judge the truth of statements in ASL. You realize that he is asking whether or not you believe the client has been telling the truth about allegations of spousal abuse.

What are the ethical issues? What are your options? What do you do and why?

CASE STUDY: Interpreting #72. During a class break, you are chatting with a Deaf student for whom you interpret. You are both signing and using no speech. Two students see you and assume you are both Deaf. One of the students makes a very rude comment about the Deaf student which you hear but of which the deaf student is unaware of.

What are the ethical issues? What are your options? What do you do and why?

CASE STUDY: Interpreting #73. You and your partner have been looking for a house. You have met a realtor and engaged in some preliminary discussions. The realtor calls and asks you to accompany a Deaf young couple on Saturday who are also in the market for a house. You agree after negotiating a fee for your services.

By the end of the day, you have seen about 15 houses — several of which you would like to look into for yourself. After the Deaf couple departs, the realtor asks what you thought about a couple of the houses, commenting that she "threw them into the tour with you in mind." One of the houses she mentions seems to be perfect for you and your partner.

What are the ethical issues? What are your options? What do you do and why?

CASE STUDY: Interpreting #74. Your company is sponsoring a Personal Financial Management seminar for employees that you attend along with some Deaf and hearing employees. You know the two individuals who are interpreting for the seminar. As you watch the interpretation, you are aware of the fact that one of the interpreters is skewing the message — consistently leaving out the option of mutual funds.

During the break you say something to the interpreter about the seminar to which this particular interpreter adds, "Yeah, but if you believe what they are saying, mutual funds are a viable option and my financial manager has warned me away from them. They are a really bad investment option." In the next segment of the seminar, you note that this interpreter continually changes the message to steer participants away from mutual funds.

What are the ethical issues? What are your options? What do you do and why?

CASE STUDY: Interpreting #75. You are working with an interpreting partner at a large banking institution where there will be an all day workshop on personality types, effective problem-solving on the job and valuing individual differences. At one point the workshop participants are instructed to complete the personality scale to determine personality type. The hearing presenter comes along and encourages the two interpreters to complete the scale as well.

Your teammate immediately takes the opportunity to complete it, while you do not. Later at break, other participants ask your teammate what type s/he was, to which the interpreter answers, sometimes signing and sometimes not. You feel this is inappropriate behavior and want to speak to your colleague about it.

What are the ethical issues? What are your options? What do you do and why?

CASE STUDY: Interpreting #76. A Deaf child (7-years old) uses a curse word to another Deaf student while playing on the playground at school. You are working as a lunch time supervisor. You know that if the two children had been speaking to each other, you would not have been able to hear them at that distance. However, you are able to see the exchange from where you stand.

What are the ethical issues? What are your options? What do you do and why?

CASE STUDY: Interpreting #77. You are working with another interpreter on an all day assignment. At break the non-initiated hearing person approaches the interpreters and Deaf person with questions about the differences between ASL and English and about deafness in general. Your interpreter partner immediately begins educating the hearing person, responding with appropriate information, signing and talking at the same time.

What are the ethical issues? What are your options? What do you do and why?

CASE STUDY: Interpreting #78. You have been working as an interpreter for a community agency for two years. In that position, you have provided professional service for a variety of clients in various settings. There is one Deaf community leader who is very challenging for you to understand. As a matter of fact, you also have difficulty understanding this individual's spouse and two Deaf children as well. For the past 12-months, you have turned down any jobs that require you to interpret for this Deaf client or members of his family. Today you are having a performance review with your supervisor in which you are to discuss your work to date, areas of needed growth and plans for professional development.

What issues might be relevant? Are there any ethical issues? What are your options? What do you do and why?

CASE STUDY: Interpreting #79. You and a second

interpreter are interpreting for an all day conference. At the
end of the morning session, the Interpreting Coordinator
approaches and states that a "working luncheon" has been
added and asks the two of you to cover it. You ask if there
are any other interpreters available and she says no.
Reluctantly, the two of you agree. During lunch, one
interpreter works while the other eats. After lunch you both
return to the conference and interpret for the closing
session. You both submit your invoices but when you
receive payment, $15.00 has been deducted from your pay
to cover the price of the lunch.

What are the ethical issues? What are your options? What
do you do and why?

CASE STUDY: Interpreting #80. You have just

graduated from an interpreting program and are looking for
your first job. You completed a job application form at the
Mulberry School District, noting your 2-year degree in
interpreting. Under the section for "certification or license"
on the form, you have written "none." When you go in for
an interview, one member of the interview panel says, "As a
certified interpreter, what contributions do you believe you
can make to our educational team?"

What are the ethical issues? What are your options? How
do you respond and why?

CASE STUDY: Interpreting #81. You are a certified interpreter with 24-years of interpreting experience under your belt. Further, you come from a Deaf family and have been signing all of your life. You don't attend any of the workshops that are offered by the local, state/provincial, or national organizations because you feel they are primarily for beginners. You only maintain your membership in the professional association in order to keep your certification active, so you never bother to read associational newsletters, current research or professional journals. When interviewed by interpreting students from the local college, you commented that while it is admirable for them to be studying interpreting they will never really use the information they are learning – especially all of the new terminology. You added that the only way to become a "master interpreter" is to grow up with Deaf people and to survive the interpreting "school of hard knocks." Reflect on the appropriateness of your behavior.

What are the ethical issues? What are the options? What might you do differently and why?

CASE STUDY: Interpreting #82. You are interpreting in a middle school for one student who has Deaf parents. One day there is a parent teacher conference that you interpret. The student is present, along with his Mother and the teacher (who does not sign). The Mom begins discussing her concerns about her son's involvement with some gangs and the impact of having an alcoholic father. You believe you are accurately interpreting what is being said but the student interrupts you repeatedly, correcting your interpretation. After a time, both the teacher and the Mother begin to question the accuracy of your work due to the son's behavior.

What are the ethical issues? What are your options? What do you do and why?

CASE STUDY: Interpreting #83. Murphy Brown works as a secretary in the local public school where you work as an interpreter. She can't read what the Deaf children at the school sign to her very well but she can put her own ideas into Sign Language. Murphy has never been trained as an interpreter. When one of the three interpreters who work for the school are absent, Murphy volunteers to interpret in their place. She has also suggested that she teach Sign Language to school staff two days per week during the lunch hour.

What are the ethical issues? What are your options? What do you do and why?

CASE STUDY: Interpreting #84. You work as a staff interpreter for the child protection agency in your city. You interpret for meetings at the office, as well as accompanying various social workers on home visits. One day you go to an apartment house with a social worker to interpret for a Deaf woman who is the court appointed custodian of her three grandchildren, one of whom is also Deaf. The children's mother is in prison. As the interview proceeds, the Grandmother complains about another daughter (the children's aunt) who lives with her. She explains that the daughter uses drugs and has sex in front of the children. The social worker excuses herself from to room to go make a telephone call. While she is out of the room, the daughter appears from a back bedroom and threatens the older woman, signing "You better get rid of them or I'm gonna kill you!" with a menacing look. The older woman looks frightened. As the daughter retreats to the bedroom, the older woman signs to you, "Shh – don't tell her (the social worker). The children and I are fine but if you tell, she might hurt me."

What are the ethical issues? What are your options? What do you do and why?

CASE STUDY: Interpreting #85. You earn your living

as an interpreter. You are asked by the Deaf community to interpret for an upcoming festival without pay. The festival will be held on Saturday which means you will have to arrange for childcare for your two children.

What are the ethical issues? What are your options? What do you do and why?

CASE STUDY: Interpreting #86. Petunia (an

experienced interpreter) has been assigned to work with you, a recent interpreting graduate. You realize immediately that you are over your head in this particular assignment. You do your best to support Petunia but are only able to handle 10 — 15 minutes at a time and really struggled with some of the concepts being discussed. After the assignment, while people were still milling around, Petunia turns to you and says, "I don't know what made you think you could do this job! You didn't convey one single idea correctly. Your incompetence caused me to do double work. You're a graduate from the interpreting program?! Believe me, I will never work with you again!"

What are the ethical issues? What are your options? What do you do and why?

CASE STUDY: Interpreting #87. You have been an interpreter for 18 years. You are well known to members of the Deaf community and a leader among the local professional interpreting association. Today, you interpreted for a disciplinary hearing at the local meat packing company involving a Deaf individual you have known for years. Upon arriving at the work site, you report to the central office where you are asked to have a seat in the waiting room. When the Deaf employee enters the office, you jump up and give her/him a big hug — a typical Deaf community greeting. The two of you are called back into the conference room where the hearing begins. When a break is called, you and the Deaf employee go outside to chat and smoke a cigarette. At the lunch break, you and the Deaf employee go together in your car to a fast food place nearby.

Reflect on this situation and identify any ethical issues. Think about your behavior and identify anything you might change and why. Explain why you would make those changes and possible implications of the changes.

CASE STUDY: Interpreting #88.   You are asked to interpret for a sports banquet at a local school. There will be 30 athletes in attendance, two of whom are Deaf. In addition, one set of parents in attendance is Deaf. It just so happens that the basketball coach is your boyfriend and the school principal is your father.

What are the ethical issues here? What are your options? Will you accept this assignment? Why or why not?

CASE STUDY: Interpreting #89.   You just moved to town from a largely rural Midwestern state where you were charging $10 per hour for legal interpreting assignments. You have not yet met members of the Deaf or interpreting community in your new location, but you have been contacted by the court to interpret for a pretrial hearing that will be held next week.

What are the ethical issues? What are your options? What do you do and why?

CASE STUDY: Interpreting #90.   You attend a meeting where the audience is made up of hearing and Deaf individuals, including some non-signing professionals. The presentation being made is regarding some recent research and complex concepts related to American Sign Language. Part of the presentation is done in spoken English (requiring interpreters to work from English into ASL) and part of the presentation is done in ASL (requiring interpreters to work from ASL into English). Several times when one of the interpreters is switching from one modality to the other, s/he makes faces or a humorous comment directed at the audience (e.g.: Hold on, gotta get my hearing head on – haha"). By the fourth time this happens, it is almost like a "side show" to the presentation. You are embarrassed and angry about the behavior – especially given the presence of interpreting students in the audience.

What are the ethical issues? What are your options? What do you do and why?

CASE STUDY: Interpreting #91. In a weekly meeting, the members of a mental health team discuss recent patient sessions, prognosis, and individual plans for treatment. Members of the team include the doctor, the psychiatric nurse, the social worker, and you — the staff interpreter. The discussion comes around to Orangutan, a Deaf patient who has just been admitted to the hospital. Because you interact with the Deaf community you have access to information via the "grapevine" that may be of significance to the discussion at hand.

What are the ethical issues? What are your options? Do you share this information? What do you do and why?

CASE STUDY: Interpreting #92. While you are interpreting for a lawyer and a Deaf individual, the Deaf client begins to talk about suicidal thoughts and extreme depression. The lawyer becomes concerned and suggests that the client seek counseling. The client replies that s/he can't do that because of the expense of the interpreting plus the counseling. As an interpreter you know there is a special program in this particular community which pays for both the therapist and the interpreting for members of the Deaf community that the lawyer and client may not know about.

What are the ethical issues? What are your options? Do you share the information you have? If so, how?

Design your own case study here.

CASE STUDIES FOR TEACHERS

CASE STUDY: Teaching #1.   You teach ASL at a City College. Based on your education, experience, and the fact that you qualified under a special earnings category agreed to in the last round of union negotiations, you are paid $ 75 per hour for teaching. The Neighborhood College 25-miles down the road pays ASL teachers $25 per hour for teaching and they have asked you to teach a class for them. You'd like to but you cannot afford to earn only $25 per hour.

One possibility is for you to teach at Neighborhood College and require students to meet at your home for two additional hours of tutoring each week for which they must pay an additional $25 per hour. That would actually mean you would earn more than $75 per hour!

What are the ethical issues here? What are your options? Is the option you have thought of ethical? What would you do and why?

CASE STUDY: Teaching #2.   You are a man and you teach at the local college. The majority of your students are young women, many of whom come to class in short skirts, tank tops and other skimpy attire. You are generally able to concentrate on your teaching and don't tend to be distracted by these physically attractive students.

Somehow the students found out that today is your birthday. They surprise you with a birthday cake in class. After class, one of your female students comes to your office to wish you a personal birthday. She gives you a card, a gift and a big hug. In the gaily wrapped package is a heart-shaped paper weight, engraved with the words "You're the best. Love, Amanda."

What are the ethical issues here? What are your options? What would you do? Why?

CASE STUDY: Teaching #3.   You have been teaching ASL for three years, having completed training in ASL linguistics, Deaf culture, and adult education. You work in a continuing education setting where several courses are taught by three different teachers. You realize that students coming into your class from Crunchie's class are not able to perform to the level expected. Their facial grammatical markers are absent and their sign repertoire is pitifully inadequate. Unfortunately this is not a one-time experience; the same pattern has occurred each semester for 18-months.

What are the ethical issues here? What are your options? Should you do/say something? If so, what and to whom? If not, why not?

CASE STUDY: Teaching #4. You have been invited to speak at a large state/provincial gathering of parents of Deaf children. Stinque's topic is related to communication strategies and interpreting services parents may encounter when their children enter public school. When you are introduced, the statement is made that you hold a doctorate in Deaf Education and have been working with families with Deaf children for 20-plus years. In actuality, you holds a Master's in Deaf Education and have been working with families with Deaf children for a little less than 10 years.

What are the ethical issues here? What are your options? Should you correct the misinformation? If so, how? If not, why not?

CASE STUDY: Teaching #5. You teach ASL and Deaf culture classes in the local interpreting program. You really enjoy this work! The students are eager to learn and you have a relaxed and comfortable relationship with them. Since you are single, you have plenty of time to meet with students after class when they need extra help or have questions. As a matter of fact, there is a bar/restaurant near the school where you often meet with students to have a drink, to share cultural information, and to "hang out."

One student this semester is particularly eager to learn. She stays after class and hangs out at the bar/restaurant with you daily. On occasion, this student has transportation problems so you take her in your car and drop her off at home.

What are the ethical issues here? Are your actions ethical? Professional? Why or why not? What might you do differently?

CASE STUDY: Teaching #6. You work as a teaching assistant with elementary age Deaf children in a mainstream setting. You attended the residential school for the Deaf as a youth but never took any postsecondary courses to prepare you for the work you do. You have never studied ASL formally, although you are a master storyteller and valued member of the Deaf community.

You have been asked to testify in an upcoming murder trial as an expert witness on the acquisition of ASL by Deaf individuals and the psychological impact of being the only Deaf member of a family.

What are the ethical issues here? What are your options? What will you answer and why?

CASE STUDY: Teaching #7. You are the head of the ASL program at the local university. You don't approve of some sign forms being used in the community and being taught in other ASL programs in the area. What can you do to address your concerns in a professional and ethical way?

CASE STUDY: Teaching #8. In this large metropolitan area, there are several colleges that teach ASL and two schools with an ASL/English interpreting program. Jezebel teaches in one of the ASL programs and you teach in one of the interpreting programs. Jezebel makes a point of telling students in her program that your program is of poor quality. She also gossips about you and the other instructors in your program to members of the Deaf community, saying that you aren't qualified to teach ASL and that you "aren't Deaf enough to be teaching ASL."

More than once, Jezebel has run into students in your interpreting program who were her former students. She commonly says, "I know you are probably unhappy in the interpreting program and I'm sure (your name) is a disappointment as a teacher. Come on, you can tell me all about it."

Identify which of Jezebel's behaviors are unethical/unprofessional. If she has legitimate concerns about teachers/programs at other institutions, what appropriate and professional actions could Jezebel take?

What are the ethical issues here? What are your options? What do you do and why?

CASE STUDY: Teaching #9. You work in a large university. You have heard that once a faculty member is tenured, "they have it made." You notice that many tenured faculty members in your Department teach classes but put in very few office hours. They also frequently skip department meetings and various committee meetings.

You will be seeking tenure next year. What ethical issues do you face? What are your options regarding work ethic as a tenured professor? What will you do and why?

CASE STUDY: Teaching #10. There is a two-year ASL Studies program at the local college and your friend encourages you to apply for a job there. You do so even though you have had no experience teaching ASL, no training in teaching adults and have never studied the grammar or structure of ASL. At the interview for the job, the committee asks, "What experience do you have teaching ASL?" You really need a job and, like most Deaf individuals, you have always taught ASL to people in your life — neighbors, friends, coworkers, hearing family members. How do you answer the question? If you were on the hiring committee, what qualifications would you expect of an ASL teacher?

CASE STUDY: Teaching #11. You are a teacher and you really enjoy your work. You have taken some workshops teaching how to develop powerful instructional materials, including making Power Point presentations, using and editing animation on your computer to create instructional videos, etc. On your own time, you have developed a set of video tapes that can be used to teach classifiers or to provide challenging practice for interpreting students.

When you show the video to some colleagues who teach at another school, they are very complimentary. One of them, a friend, asks if he can borrow the video to study more closely and give you some additional ideas/feedback. You happily agree.

He returns the video a couple of weeks later but never gives you any kind of critique. Then you hear that students in your friend's school have seen your videotape. There is only one explanation: your friend copied the tape without your permission and has been using it in his classes.

What are the ethical issues in this situation? What would you do and why? Do you say something to your friend? If so, what?

CASE STUDY: Teaching #12. You have been teaching for a number of years. It so happenes that a university in another state contacts you and asks you to be part of a program review committee. This means you will go to their school, review their curriculum, observe some classes, interview students, and provide the university with a written critique of their program along with suggestions for changes.

While on site, you are observing a class when the teacher gives students several handouts. As a courtesy, the teacher gives you a copy. As you look over the handouts, you recognize two of them as documents you have developed and used in classes and workshops. There is no citation giving you credit as the originator of the documents.

What ethical issues arise in this situation? Would you speak to the teacher about this? Would your opinion of the university program be influenced as a result of your discovery? What would you do and why?

CASE STUDY: Teaching #13. You share an office with another instructor in the program. She is very unhappy about a number of things in the school. She has no respect for the Dean — "he just isn't that bright!" She thinks the program coordinator is too soft — "She is a push over! Our program will never get the resources it needs because she doesn't have the courage to fight for it." She is critical of other teachers in the program — "So-and-so is totally inept as a teacher!"

You can't get much work done in the office because every time you are in, she steals your time complaining about everyone and every thing. You also observe her speaking disparagingly about others to students who come to the office.

What are the ethical issues here? What are your options? What do you do and why?

CASE STUDY: Teaching #14. When grading papers submitted by students, you realize three of the papers are practically identical. When you go back to check them, you compare several sections of each paper with one of the resource books. Obviously, these three students copied each other's work and plagiarized large sections from the book in question.

One of the students has been struggling with her assignments. If she fails this one, she will flunk out of the program. She is a nice woman, a single Mom who has been struggling with a disabled child. You really like her and don't want to see her fail.

What are the ethical issues here? What are your options? What do you do and why?

CASE STUDY: Teaching #15. You and your colleague share an office. On more than one occasion, you have found your papers moved and things on your desk in a different arrangement than where you left them. There have been times when you reached for a book or videotape from your bookshelf, only to find it missing. You have spoken to your office mate about this. He has admitted to borrowing a book or tape from time to time but insists that he never bothers your desk or papers.

Today when you came in, you discover that a confidential file you had is missing from your desk drawer. When you look about the office in search of it, you see if lying on your office mate's desk.

What are the ethical issues here? What are your options? What do you do and why?

CASE STUDY: Teaching #16. You teach at the local college and are engaged to be married. Your fiancé works as an administrative assistant to the President of a large bank.

Shortly after your marriage, your spouse decides to quit work and return to school. Much to your surprise, s/he decides to study ASL/English interpretation, the program in which you teach.

What are the ethical issues here? What are your options? What do you do and why?

CASE STUDY: Teaching #17. There is a student in your class — approximately your age — whom you like quite a bit. She is bright, witty and dedicated to her studies. At the class break, you sometimes go outside with the smokers in your class, one of whom is this particular student.

There are times when this student asks to meet with you alone during the break to discuss something related to the class or the Deaf community. You are beginning to think of this individual as a friend and colleague.

What are the ethical issues here? What are your options? What do you do and why?

CASE STUDY: Teaching #18. You and the other faculty members in your department meet to discuss the schedule of classes to be offered next semester. Each course is listed with the day and time. After lengthy discussion, each teacher agrees to teach a set of four classes.

Early in the month when classes are supposed to begin, you realize you have a conflict and cannot teach the Wednesday evening session of a class that is to meet Monday-Wednesday evenings. You are torn. If you contact the program coordinator, s/he will probably assign the whole class to someone else, which will mean a loss of income to you. You could teach the Monday evening sessions and ask a friend to teach the Wednesday evening sessions. You could pay your friend "under the table," that way you would not lose the class.

What are the ethical issues here? What are your options? What do you do and why?

CASE STUDY: Teaching #19. You have been charged with the responsibility of redesigning the curriculum for two courses in the program within which you teach. You accepted the job with excitement and the intent to give it your best effort. However, your work is due at the end of the following week and there is no way you will be able to complete it on time.

You have a friend in another state/province and you are aware that s/he has just completed similar work. You could complete the task on time if you submitted your friend's work as your own.

What are the ethical issues here? What are your options? What do you do and why?

CASE STUDY: Teaching #20. You have some very strong philosophical beliefs regarding ASL, Deaf culture, oppression and oralism. Another faculty member takes an opposing stance on virtually every issue. Your department is now advertising for a new faculty member and you are both on the screening committee. One of the candidates to be interviewed is from the same school of thought as your colleague.

What are the ethical issues here? What are your options? What do you do and why?

CASE STUDY: Teaching #21. You require students to contact you in advance if they will be absent from class. Your course outline states, "Students are required to call my office prior to the beginning of class if they are unable to attend. If you do not have a TTY, you will have to call via the relay system."

You are now facing two problems. Students are sometimes calling your hearing office mate to leave a voice message regarding their absence, asking the hearing instructor to pass the message on to you. In addition, one student is calling you at home to advise you of an absence or to ask you questions about class.

What are the issues here? What are your options? What do you do and why?

CASE STUDY: Teaching #22. You teach part-time evenings and weekends. To date, childcare has not been a problem. However, this afternoon when you stopped by your babysitter's place to drop off your five-year old, she came to the door in her pajamas — obviously quite ill. She apologizes but says she cannot take your child. Class will begin in 45-minutes. You have no family or friends in the area to turn to.

What are the issues here? What are your options? What do you do and why?

CASE STUDY: Teaching #23. You have prepared feedback for students based on their recent skills exam. Several of the students did quite well, but three students failed miserably.

You have designed your class plan to return the exams and give general feedback. Next you plan to divide the class into smaller working groups while you meet individually with the three students who failed the exam.

When you arrive in class, there is a stranger sitting among the students. When you inquire, you are told it is the cousin of one of the failing students who is visiting from out of town.

What are the ethical issues here? What are your options? What do you do and why?

CASE STUDY: Teaching #24. You have lots of ideas about how to expand and improve the educational program in your school. You would like to see more classes offered, the introduction of more teachers so students have a greater variety of language and interpreting models. You have discussed your ideas with two other teachers and they are very supportive. You decide to write up your proposal and forward it to the Board of Directors of the college. In addition, plan to go to the Deaf club this weekend and explain your plan. You will ask the members of the Deaf club to join you in a demonstration rally at the next meeting of the College Board of Directors. You and others will make posters, call the media, and insist that the college implement your plan.

What are the ethical issues here? What are your options? What do you do and why?

CASE STUDY: Teaching #25. You are a busy person! You hold down a full-time job and teach part-time three nights a week. You also have a family and are an active member of local Deaf/interpreting organizations. When your schedule is tight, you tend to "steal time" away from your class preparations, after all you have taught these courses before and can "wing it" if necessary.

What are the ethical issues here? What are your options? What do you do and why?

CASE STUDY: Teaching #26. You are a certified interpreter teaching in the interpreting program. You maintain an active freelance practice as well. The program requires students to complete a minimum number of observation hours in their first semester. You have interpreting work in the upcoming week including (a) a two-day trial, (b) a large meeting for a multi-level marketing business, (c) two medical appointments, and (d) a job interview. You would like to offer students an opportunity to observe your work.

What are the ethical issues here? What are your options? What do you do and why?

CASE STUDY: Teaching #27. The educational program at your college/university is currently advertising a position for a new instructor and you chair the search committee. Your have been involved with someone who lives some distance away for several years. Your "significant other" decides to apply for the job.

What are the ethical issues here? What are your options? What do you do and why?

CASE STUDY: Teaching #28. You have just been hired as a part-time instructor at the local college. They have given you copies of the syllabus and course outlines but you don't understand everything on the documents. You decide not to bother with it; you will just "do your own thing."

What are the ethical issues here? What are your options? What do you do and why?

CASE STUDY: Teaching #29. Your co-worker is consistently late to her classes, arrives unprepared, and spends most of her class time telling students about her personal life and problems. You are aware of these things both from personal observation and from complaints made to you by students. You know the program coordinator and the Dean know nothing about what is happening.

What are the ethical issues here? What are your options? What do you do and why?

CASE STUDY: Teaching #30. At the request of your supervisor, you wrote a grant for funds to set up a special program in educational interpreting. Much to your delight, the grant was approved and your school has been awarded $500,000 for this two-year project.

While you felt competent in the writing of the grant, you do not believe you are the most qualified to actually work on the project. However, your supervisor insists that you become the project coordinator, working on it full-time.

What are the ethical issues here? What are your options? What do you do and why?

Design your own case study here.

Appendix C

Sample Codes of Ethics and Professional Standards

Sample Codes of Ethics and Professional Standards

- ❖ **Psychiatric Nurses Association of Canada**
  Code of Ethics

- ❖ **The Society of Translators and Interpreters of British Columbia**
  Code of Ethics

- ❖ **American Sign Language Teachers Association**
  Code of Ethics

- ❖ **Camosun College**
  Professional Guidelines for Teachers

- ❖ **American Mental Health Counselors Association**   Standards for the Clinical Practice of Mental Health Counseling

- ❖ **Registry of Interpreters for the Deaf**
  Code of Ethics

- ❖ **Association of Visual Language Interpreters of Canada**
  Code of Ethics

PSYCHIATRIC NURSES ASSOCIATION OF CANADA

CODE OF ETHICS

The Code of Ethics is established to provide moral standards for the ethical behavior of the profession and to provide direction to Registered Psychiatric Nurses for ethical decision-making in Psychiatric Nursing practice.

The Psychiatric Nurses Association of Canada expects its members shall abide by the Code of Ethics as a condition of initial and continued membership.

The core values embedded in and woven throughout this Code of Ethics includes duties related to:

- ❖ Accountability

- ❖ Responsible Caring

- ❖ Integrity in Relationships

- ❖ Professional Responsibilities

- ❖ Responsibility to Society

ACCOUNTABILITY

Psychiatric Nurses demonstrate accountability through the application of human values in Psychiatric Nursing.

Psychiatric Nurses are responsible to promote mental health by providing individualized and holistic prevention, treatment and rehabilitation services.

Psychiatric Nurses promote confidence in all members of the interdisciplinary health team and as such are responsible to report unethical practice.

RESPONSIBLE CARING

Psychiatric Nurses demonstrate an active concern for the well being of any individuals with whom they relate in a professional role.

Psychiatric Nurses recognize that caring is a holistic process.

Psychiatric Nurses respect the uniqueness and integrity of individuals and do not discriminate on the basis of color; race; gender; age; personal beliefs and practices or social status.

INTEGRITY IN RELATIONSHIPS

Psychiatric Nurses demonstrate responsible caring and acknowledge and respect the dignity and autonomy of every individual.

Psychiatric Nurses hold in high regard the need to assure the confidentiality of information regarding the individual and the treatment they receive.

Psychiatric Nurses acknowledge and respect the autonomy and privacy of individuals in relationships.

PROFESSIONAL RESPONSIBILITIES

Psychiatric Nurses, as professionals, are expected to maintain standards of personal conduct which reflect credit upon the profession.

Psychiatric Nurses will maintain current theoretical and clinical knowledge and will enhance that knowledge through continuing education and evidence based practice. They will practice in areas where they have professional skills and will identify and maintain an awareness of professional and personal limitations.

Psychiatric Nurses recognize, respect and collaborate with appropriate others.

Psychiatric Nurses demonstrate professional judgment and accept responsibility for professional judgments in practice. They will demonstrate honesty and integrity to avoid situations of conflict of interest.

RESPONSIBILITY TO SOCIETY/PUBLIC GOOD

Psychiatric Nurses are responsible to maintain public confidence and trust and will thereby act in the best interests of the public, provided that is not to the detriment of the individual.

Psychiatric Nurses will not participate in the public promotion of any products and/or services which do not reflect positively on the profession of Psychiatric Nursing.

February 1998

The Society of Translators and Interpreters of British Columbia

CODE OF ETHICS

PRINCIPLES

In this code, unless otherwise stated, "member" shall refer to translators, interpreters and terminologists belonging to the Society, whether certified or associate.

❖   Members shall abide by the Code of Ethics and shall be answerable to the Society for any breach thereof.

❖   Members shall accept full responsibility for the quality of their work.

❖   Members shall accept an assignment only if they are well qualified with respect to knowledge of both languages involved and the skills required, and only if the subject matter is within their competence.

❖   Members shall refrain from making misleading statements regarding their level of competence or their certification. In their advertising, they shall clearly indicate their certification in terms of languages and professional class (translator, court interpreter, conference interpreter, terminologist). Only Certified Members of the Society may use the term "Certified Member" or "Member" on business cards, letterhead, professional advertising in general or on publications of which they are the author or translator.

❖   Certified Members may also use the term "Certified Translator," "Certified Court Interpreter," "Certified Conference Interpreter" or "Certified Terminologist" as appropriate.

❖   Associate Members who wish to mention their membership in the Society shall use the term "Associate Member."

❖   Members shall refrain from unfair tactics in the practice of their profession.

❖ Members shall act towards colleagues in a spirit of mutual cooperation as well as assist and encourage beginners in the profession.

❖ Where applicable, members shall respect all copyrights and other intellectual property rights.

❖ Members shall not divulge privileged information.

❖ Members shall not use their professional role to perform functions that lie beyond the scope of a language professional, such as advocacy, counseling or improper disclosure of information.

❖ When interpreting in the courts of British Columbia, members shall abide by the Code of Professional Conduct established for court interpreters by the Ministry of Attorney General.

❖ The Society members' professional seal shall be obtained only through application to the Society and shall be used only by Certified Members in good standing.

American Sign Language Teachers Association

CODE OF ETHICS

Principle #1: Content Competence   *A teacher of ASL/Deaf Studies maintains a high level of language/subject matter knowledge and ensures that course content is current, accurate, representative, and appropriate to the level of the course within students' program of study.*

GUIDELINES: This principle means that a teacher of ASL/Deaf Studies is responsible for maintaining subject matter competence not only in areas of personal interest, but in all areas relevant to a course's goals or objectives. The teacher is responsible for teaching content as stated in the course syllabus and for adequately preparing students for subsequent courses.

Failure to fulfill this principle occurs when a teacher (1) deliberately misrepresents his/her or another's professional qualifications, (2) accepts employment/agrees to teach a course for which he/she has inadequate knowledge, (3) misinterprets research evidence to support a theory or social view favored by the instructor, (4) teaches only those topics in the course in which he/she has a personal interest or (5) does not provide adequate representation of alternate points of view regarding a topic.

Principle #2: Teaching/Pedagogical Competence
A pedagogically competent teacher is knowledgeable regarding alternative instructional methods or strategies, and selects methods of instruction that, according to research evidence (including personal or self-reflective research), is effective in helping students to learn and to achieve the course objectives.

GUIDELINES: This principle means that not only do ASL/Deaf Studies teachers have the requisite knowledge and skills in the content area, American Sign Language and/or Deaf Studies, but they also must demonstrate adequate pedagogical skills to be able to select effective instructional methods, provide practice and feedback opportunities and to accommodate student diversity. This principle implies that the teacher recognizes the differences in teaching a group of interpreting students in a college setting versus teaching parents of Deaf students or interested persons in a community setting. In teaching a beginning course in ASL, the teacher provides students with adequate opportunity to practice and receive feedback on their receptive and expressive skills during the course. The teacher is responsible for taking active steps to stay current regarding teaching strategies that will help students learn. This might mean reading literature related to ASL and/or Deaf Studies teaching, attending workshops and conferences, or experimentation with alternative methods of teaching.

Principle #3: Dealing with Alternative Points of View *For topics involving difference of opinion or interpretation, teachers of ASL/Deaf Studies take active steps to acknowledge, respect, and place in perspective alternative points of view that are representative of various segments of the Deaf community.*

GUIDELINES: This principle means that teachers do not deny students access to different points of view regarding topics sensitive to the Deaf community nor points of view which are different than the teacher's own. A teacher of ASL/Deaf Studies takes precaution to distinguish between his/her personal views and those in current practice in the field. The teacher identifies his/her own perspective on a topic and compares it to alternative views/interpretations, thereby providing students with an understanding of the complexity of the issue and the difficulty of achieving a single "objective" conclusion, or a conclusion representative of the entire Deaf community.

Teachers are responsible for sharing information related to Deaf people, their identities, their language choices, and their cultures in an open and professional manner, refraining from making negative remarks about any member of that community, whatever his/her language choices/preferences may be. Within this context, teachers should be aware of the situational specific use of language and model respect and sensitivity for the diversity of language usage within the Deaf community.

Failure to fulfill this principle occurs when a teacher: disagrees with the use of particular signs or means of signing used by some members of the Deaf community; makes negative remarks, disparages or causes students to disparage or acquire negative views of those segments of the Deaf community.

Principle#4: Equitable Treatment of all Students *The teacher of ASL/Deaf Studies shall accord equitable treatment for all students.*

GUIDELINES: The overriding responsibility of the teacher is to contribute to the student's development of competence and skill in the use of ASL and knowledge of Deaf culture and to avoid actions that could detract from student development. This principle means that the teacher must provide instruction that facilitates learning and encourages autonomy and independent thinking in students and treats all students with respect and dignity. The teacher of ASL/Deaf Studies encourages students to be respectful not only of all segments of the Deaf community, but of one another as well. In order to provide an inclusive and open environment for class discussion, the teacher acknowledges alternative points of view within the classroom, avoid behavior which could be perceived as coercing students to adopt a particular value or point of view, encouraging students to express alternate points of view, and modeling respect for all students even when it is necessary to disagree.

Principle #5: Relationships with Students *A teacher of ASL/Deaf Studies should not engage in a course of conduct that encourages development of any but professional relationships between themselves and students.*

GUIDELINES: This principle means that it is the responsibility of the teacher to keep relationships with students focused on the instructional goal of developing competence and skill in ASL and/or Deaf Studies. To avoid conflict of interest, a teacher does not enter into dual-role relationships with students that are likely to detract from student development or lead to actual or perceived favoritism on the part of the teacher.

The most obvious example of a dual relationship that is likely to impair teacher objectivity and/or detract from student development is any form of sexual or close personal relationship with a current student. It is the responsibility of the ASL/Deaf Studies teacher to be aware of the power differential between themselves and students and to avoid behaving in ways that could exploit that relationship.

Other potentially problematic dual relationships include accepting a teaching (or grading) role with respect to a member of one's immediate family or a close friend, excessive socializing with individual students outside of class, and introducing a course requirement that students participate in a cultural or political movement advocated by the teacher.

Although there are definite benefits to establishing good rapport with students and interacting with students both inside and outside the classroom, there are also risks of exploitation. It is the responsibility of the ASL/Deaf Studies teacher to prevent these risks from materializing into real or perceived conflicts of interests.

Principle #6: Confidentiality *Student grades, attendance records, and private communications are treated as confidential materials and are released only with student consent or for legitimate academic purposes.*

GUIDELINES: This principle suggests that students are entitled to the same level of confidentiality in their relationships with teachers as would exist in a lawyer-client or doctor-patient relationship. Whatever rules or policies are followed with respect to confidentiality of student records, these should be disclosed in full to students at the beginning of the academic term.

Principle #7: Respect for Colleagues *An ASL/Deaf Studies teacher accords just and equitable treatment for all members of the profession, respects the dignity of colleagues, and works cooperatively with them in the interest of fostering student development and the profession of ASL/Deaf Studies teaching.*

GUIDELINE: This principle means that in interactions among colleagues with respect to teaching and teaching competence, the overriding concern is the development of students. An ASL/Deaf Studies teacher should not intentionally make a false or malicious statement about a colleague's professional performance or conduct. Any kind of derogatory statement regarding another's competence in the presence of students is unacceptable. Disagreements between teachers related to teaching are settled privately. If a teacher suspects that a colleague has shown incompetence or ethical violations in teaching, the teacher takes responsibility for investigating the matter thoroughly and consulting privately with the colleague and/or appropriate supervisory personnel.

A specific example of failure to show respect for colleagues occurs when a teacher makes derogatory comments in the classroom about the competence of another teacher or group of teachers. For example, "A" tells students that information provided to them by teacher "B" is of no use or incorrect and will be replaced by information from teacher "A." Other examples of failure to uphold this principle would be for teacher "A" to discourage students from taking a course from teacher "B," who is disliked by teacher "A," even though the course would be useful.

Principle #8: Valid Assessment of Students *Teachers of ASL/Deaf Studies are responsible for taking adequate steps to ensure that testing/assessment of students is valid, open, fair, and in agreement with course objectives.*

GUIDELINES: This principle means that whether the teacher is teaching an ASL/Deaf Studies course to adults in the community or a university course required in an academic program, he/she selects assessment techniques that are consistent with the objectives of the course and at the same time are as reliable and valid as possible. Testing procedures and grading standards should be communicated to students at the beginning of the course and followed throughout. Students should be provided with prompt and accurate feedback on their performance at regular intervals throughout the course with an explanation as to how their work was graded. The teacher should provide students with constructive suggestions as to how to improve their grades.

One example of an inappropriate testing practice would be to grade students on skills that were not part of the announced course objectives and/or were not given adequate practice opportunity during the course. Another violation occurs when teachers teaching two different sections of the same course use drastically different testing procedures or grading standards, such that the same level of student performance earns significantly different final grades in the two sections.

Principle #9: Respect for the Profession of ASL/Deaf Studies Teaching   *A teacher of ASL/Deaf Studies should conduct him/herself in such a manner as to bring respect to themselves, their students, and the profession and shall strive to maintain high professional standards in compliance with the Code of Ethics.*

GUIDELINES: A teacher of ASL/Deaf Studies should be knowledgeable regarding fees appropriate to the profession and be informed about the suggested fee schedule of the national organization, There may be circumstances when an instructor elects to provide instruction in a community setting free of charge or for a nominal fee. This should be done with discretion taking care that the livelihood of other teachers who must charge for their instructional services will be protected.

Principle #10: Respect for Institution   *In the interests of student development, a teacher is aware of and respects the educational goals, policies and standards of the institution or community setting in which he/she teaches.*

GUIDELINES: This principle implies that a teacher shares a collective responsibility to work for the good of the employing body as a whole, to uphold its educational goals and standards and to abide by its policies and regulations.

Adopted 1998

STATEMENT OF
PROFESSIONAL STANDARDS

The following statement was developed at Camosun College (Victoria, B.C.) and is a part of each contract signed by teachers offering courses through their Continuing Education program.

As an instructor you will:

1.1   Possess and develop current knowledge and skills in your content area.

1.2   Possess and develop professional qualifications as required.

1.3   Possess current knowledge and skills in adult education, including the ability to:

    1.3.1   Describe the characteristics of the adult learner:

    1.3.2   Assess individual learner's needs and adapt course materials to these needs;

    1.3.3   Design course materials, which include lesson plans and learning objectives;

    1.3.4   Establish a safe physical and social environment that supports learning;

1.3.5   Demonstrate and maintain instructional competence in order to facilitate effective learning, using a variety of teaching methods;

1.3.6   Demonstrate skill in interpersonal and group communication; and

1.3.7   Measure learning, informally and formally.

1.4   Maintain an ethical and impartial position by not promoting, soliciting or selling any product, service or supplier, whether or not you stand to make a personal gain.

1.5   Refer queries for additional similar instructional services to your Portfolio Manager for follow-up.

1.6   Present a professional and positive image as a representative of Camosun College by being well prepared, organized and supportive.

1.7   Be responsible for fulfilling the administrative responsibilities outlined in the Instructor Guide.

1.8   Respect the confidentiality of the class list provided and recognize that it remains the property of the College.

1.9   Ensure that information discussed/disclosed in the classroom is kept confidential.

American Mental Health Counselors Association

STANDARDS FOR THE CLINICAL PRACTICE OF MENTAL HEALTH COUNSELING

A.   Standards of Profession

Mental health counselors who deliver clinical services shall comply with established standards of the profession.

COMMENT: National standards for the clinical practice of mental health counseling require the counselor to have a minimum of a master's degree and a total of 60 graduate semester hours consisting of a 48-hour core curriculum, with 12 hours in a mental health counseling; clinical counseling practicum; and clinical counseling internship.

Mental health counselors who deliver clinical services must document a minimum of 3,000 hours of supervised post-graduate clinical experience over at least a two-year period including a minimum of 200 hours of face-to-face supervision. Clinical experience is defined as the direct delivery of counseling to clients as clients, involving the presence of a diagnosed mental disorder as defined by the current edition of the *Diagnostic and Statistical Manual*, or *International Classification of Diseases, Clinical Modification.*

In addition, they must adhere to ethical standards established by the profession, submit an acceptable clinical work sample, pass the national clinical mental health counselor examination, adhere to the profession's standard for clinical practice, and where available, be licensed by the state licensing board at the clinical level of practice.

B.   Statutory Regulations

Mental health counselors who deliver clinical services shall comply with local statutory regulations which govern the practice of clinical mental health counseling.

COMMENT: Mental health counselors who deliver clinical services must be aware of and adhere to all state laws governing the practice of clinical mental health counseling. In addition, they must be aware of and adhere to all administrative rules and regulations, ethical standards, and other requirements of state clinical mental health counseling or related regulatory boards. Counselors must obtain competent legal advice concerning interpretation of and compliance with all relevant statutes and regulations.

In the absence of state laws governing the practice of counseling, mental health counselors who wish to deliver clinical services must adhere strictly to the American Mental Health Counselors Association's *Standards for Clinical Practice of Mental Health Counseling.* Counselors must obtain competent legal advice concerning interpretation of and compliance with these standards.

C.   Codes of Ethics

Mental health counselors who deliver clinical services shall comply with established codes of ethics for the specific practice of clinical mental health counseling.

COMMENT: Mental health counselors who deliver clinical services are responsible first to society, second to consumers, third to the profession, and last, to themselves. Clinical mental health counselors identify themselves as members of the counseling profession. They must adhere to the codes of ethics of the American Counseling Association, American Mental Health Counselors Association, the Clinical Mental Health Academy of the National Board of Certified Counselors. They also must adhere to ethical standards endorsed by state boards regulating counseling, and cooperate fully with the adjudication procedures of ethics committees, peer review teams, and appropriate state boards.

All clinical mental health counselors must willingly participate in a formal review of their clinical work, as needed. The will provide to clients appropriate information on filing complaints alleging unethical behavior.

D.   Continuing Education

Mental health counselors who deliver clinical services shall have and maintain a repertoire of specialized counseling skills and participate in a continuing education program to enhance specialized knowledge of the practice of clinical mental health counseling.

COMMENT: Mental health counselors who deliver clinical services must have knowledge of human behavior necessary for effective diagnosis and treatment of individuals, families, and groups. (12 academic areas are listed)

To maintain and enhance skills, and acquire additional knowledge, mental health counselors who deliver clinical services must actively participate in a formal professional development and continuing education program. A minimum of 25 contact hours per year must be documented.

E.   Responsiveness

Mental health counselors who deliver clinical services shall respond in a professional manner to all who seek their services.

COMMENT: Clinical mental health counselors must provide services to each client requesting services regardless of lifestyle, origin, race, color, age, handicap, sex, religion, or sexual orientation, They must be knowledgeable and sensitive to cultural diversity and the multicultural issues of clients.

However, clinical mental health counselors must limit their services to clients whom they have the knowledge, skills, and resources to assist. When they cannot meet the needs of a particular client for any reason, clinical mental health counselors must do what is necessary to ensure the client is put in contact with an appropriate mental health counselor.

Timely appointments must be available to all clients. Mental health counselors who deliver clinical services must determine the urgency of the client's situation and be available to see the client when needed to ensure the welfare of the client. If counselors are not available to see clients when needed, it is their responsibility to assist clients in finding an appropriate and timely resource ...

When clients elect to terminate treatment and seek help elsewhere, counselors must facilitate continuity of care by providing records, upon written request, to new counselors or therapists without delay. Counselors will cooperate fully in completing the transition.

Clinical mental health counselors must not disparage the qualifications of colleagues. Neither may they claim skills superior to those of colleagues for any reason.

F.   Accessibility

Mental health counselors who deliver clinical services shall be accessible to clients.

COMMENT: Mental health counselors who deliver clinical services must be available to clients at all times. The unscheduled needs of clients will be handled through personal answering services or by answering machines. Telephone calls must be checked on a regular basis and returned promptly, accurately, and in a respectful manner. When out of town, on vacation, ill or otherwise unavailable, mental health counselors who deliver clinical services must make arrangements for coverage by competent professionals.

Offices of clinical mental health counselors must be accessible by public transportation, where available. Their office space must be easily accessible to the handicapped.

G.   Accurate Representation

Mental health counselors who deliver clinical services shall accurately represent themselves to consumers.

COMMENT: All information concerning clinical mental health counselors, services available, and related activities must be truthful, accurate, and complete, to assist prospective clients in making informed judgments and choices on matters of concern.

Mental health counselors who deliver clinical services must limit personal information to name; highest relevant degree conferred from a regionally accredited institution of higher learning; state licensure, certification or registration, including number; address, telephone number, office hours; brief explanation of types of services offered, types of problems dealt with, and cost of services.

Clinical mental health counselors must not refer to degrees earned from non-regionally accredited colleges and universities, or outside the field of counseling, that is, in administration, physical education, or other unrelated fields. Neither may they for any reason fail to state the relevant terminal degree designation after their name.

Clinical mental health counselors must indicate clearly their clinical certification status, and not imply endorsement by a clinical certification body unless in possession of a formal document attesting to full clinical certification, eligibility, or equivalency ...

Clinical mental health counselors may announce membership in or affiliation with professional organizations, associations, and agencies. For example, clinical mental health counselors may choose to announce professional membership in the American Counseling Association, American Mental Health Counselors Association, and the International Society for the Study of Multiple Personality Association. However, clinical mental health counselors *may not imply endorsement* of personal professional services by any professional entities.

Mental health counselors who deliver clinical services must not announce or imply possession of unique skills beyond those available to others in the profession ...

H.   Confidentiality

Mental health counselors who deliver clinical services shall protect the confidentiality of clients.

COMMENT: Trust between clinical mental health counselors and their clients is an essential ingredient of the counseling process. Therefore, except when explicit, overriding circumstances require, mental health counselors who deliver clinical services must not share relevant information concerning clients without their written and informed consent. In situations where reporting is required by law, clinical mental health counselors must fully inform clients of the exceptions to confidentiality, advise them fully of information that will be shared, and handle the feelings evoked. Such situations include suspected child sexual abuse and disclosures necessary for the safety and personal well-being of the client, such as a child's self-destructive behavior or an adult's overt threat to kill someone.

All soft and hard copy materials related to clients must be considered official records and maintained so as to be useful to mental health counselors treating clients. They also must be handled so as to ensure the privacy and confidentiality of clients and the integrity of all counseling materials. Information concerning clients is not available to anyone without clients' fully informed and written consent. Provision must be made for destruction of all or parts of official records when the data is no longer useful. No part of official records may be destroyed after clients request data or courts request information concerning clients.

I.   Office Procedures

Mental health counselors who deliver clinical services shall develop and adhere to consistent office procedures.

COMMENT: Clinical mental health counselors must establish and adhere to consistent office policies and procedures. They should obtain a legal opinion on them and refer to such opinion, as needed.

Professional disclosure material must be created and regularly updated.

Standard procedures for collecting and maintaining data on clients must be established and followed. All records must be maintained accurately, without bias or prejudice, and handled in a safe and secure manner. Records must be made available to clients upon request. Clinical mental health counselors must discuss with clients the implications of the materials before they are shared.

Clinical mental health counselors must maintain appropriate professional liability insurance, premises accident liability insurance, and any other insurance appropriate for protection of both counselors and clients.

Fee schedules, billing procedures, and collection procedures must be established and followed throughout the course of treatment. Should changes be necessary clients must be informed of such changes in advance ...

J.   Peer Review, Supervision and Consultation

Mental health counselors who deliver clinical services shall maintain a program of peer review, supervision and consultation.

COMMENT: Clinical mental health counselors must create and maintain an on-going program for receiving feedback about their work from other mental health professionals.

In the process of acquiring the first 3,000 hours of client contact in postgraduate clinical experience, beginning clinical mental health counselors must obtain supervision at the rate of one hour of face-to-face supervision for every fifteen (15) hours of client contact, up to the required 200 hours of supervision.

After the first 3,000 hours of client contact, the ratio of supervision to client contact hours may be reduced to include a minimum of one (1) hour of face-to-face supervision for every 30 hours of face-to-face contact with clients. However, it is expected clinical mental health counselors will seek additional supervision as determined by the needs of individual clients, as difficulties beyond the normal range of expectation are perceived by supervisors, and as recommendations for additional supervision are made by supervisors.

Experienced clinical mental health counselors with the equivalent of five years of full-time supervised clinical work may elect supervision on an as needed basis. Need is to be determined by individual counselors; however, clinical mental health counselors must ensure a minimal but optimum level of consultation and supervision ...

K.   Mental Health Continuum

Mental health counselors who deliver clinical services shall understand and utilize the continuum of mental health care.

COMMENT: Clinical mental health counselors must know, accept, and acknowledge the limit and uncertainties of current mental health treatment knowledge and techniques. Furthermore, they must be aware of the limits of their knowledge and techniques and must not practice outside the scope of their individual education, training, experience, national certification, licensure, certification or registration for any reason.

Clinical mental health counselors must acknowledge when their services are no longer benefiting a client or are beyond the scope of their education, training, experience, national certification, or statutory regulation, and must make this known to clients and other responsible parties. Thereafter, clinical mental health counselors must terminate treatment and make a referral to the appropriate resource. Should clients not wish to be referred, the counseling relationship must be terminated so as not to inhibit seeking assistance in the future.

L.   Independent Practice

Mental health counselors who deliver clinical services have the right to establish an independent practice.

COMMENT: Clinical mental health counselors must be qualified for private or independent practice, whether full-time or on a limited basis while employed elsewhere. In both limited practice and full-time practice clinical mental health counselors are responsible for assuring that all clinical services, including diagnosis and treatment, provided by themselves, employees, consultants and others meet national standards for the clinical practice of mental health counseling.

Employed mental health counselors who deliver clinical services must not use their employment setting to establish or maintain a limited independent practice or to establish a full-time practice. For example, a clinical mental health counselor will not refer paying clients to themselves nor have the employing agency refer clients to their practice.

Prior to leaving an employment setting to enter independent practice, clinical mental health counselors must begin termination with clients in a timely manner. They must obtain written approval of a termination procedure that offers clients the following options: terminating treatment; remaining in treatment at the present setting and being transferred to another staff member; transferring to another professional outside the present setting or continuing with the present clinical mental health counselor in the independent practice setting. Options must be discussed with clients in the presence of an agency staff member and all clients must be offered the same options ...

M.   Qualification to Practice

Mental health counselors who deliver clinical services shall engage in the independent practice of clinical mental health counseling only when qualified to do so.

COMMENT: Most states regulate counselors. If mental health counselors who deliver clinical services practice in such states, they must be licensed in order to engage in independent practice. If a clinical license is available, they must be licensed at that level ...

N.   Service Environment

Mental health counselors who deliver clinical services shall provide clients with a wholesome environment in which to receive services.

COMMENT: Clinical mental health counselors must ensure a reasonable degree of safety and comfort for their clients. They must take reasonable steps to assure the personal security of clients and themselves. Parking lots must be well lighted. The office space where services are rendered must be free of distractions and must be quiet and private. Waiting rooms and offices must be kept clean. Restroom facilities must be available and well-maintained. The area outside the office building must be clean and safe. The office must be easily accessible to the handicapped.

O.   Advocacy

Mental health counselors who deliver clinical services shall assume the social responsibility of advocating for their clients.

COMMENT: Clinical mental health counselors must actively support public and private programs benefiting persons with mental and emotional problems and conducive to prevention and early intervention. They must be visible in local, state, regional and national mental health associations, and support legislation for prevention, early intervention and diagnosis and treatment of mental and emotional disorders.

Clinical mental health counselors must be knowledgeable of available community-based service and resources. They must work toward gaining entry for clients in all needed community or school-based resources. Referrals will be made to meet the clients' needs. Clinical mental health counselors must serve as client advocates in order to obtain optimal benefits from needed resources.

Clinical mental health counselors must work in collaboration with other community-based providers with whom clients have contact ...

P. Reimbursement for Services

Mental health counselors who deliver clinical services shall be considered competent to receive reimbursement from all available payment systems for services rendered.

COMMENT: Mental health counselors who deliver clinical services are qualified to be compensated for their services in all ways currently available to psychiatrists, clinical psychologists, clinical social workers, psychiatric nurses, and marriage and family therapists. Mechanisms of compensation include cash, credit cards and third-party payments through health maintenance organizations; preferred provider programs; employee assistance programs; business coalitions; contractual arrangements with local, state, and national mental health and rehabilitation programs; contractual arrangements with departments of human services and human resources ...

Q. Evaluation of Effectiveness

Mental health counselors who deliver clinical services shall evaluate the effectiveness of their services.

COMMENT: Clinical mental health counselors must collect data on their delivery of services, to be used in modifying client treatment goals and strategies, and directing the individual counselor's plan for professional and personal growth and development. Evaluation begins with the initial interview of the client, and continues through case development plan (including client input) and execution of the treatment plan ...

R.   Counselor Issues and Impairment

Mental health counselors who deliver clinical services shall be aware of anything which might interfere with their effectiveness and shall refrain from any activity which might lead to inadequate performance or harm to anyone, including themselves and clients.

COMMENT: Clinical mental health counselors must be aware of personal problems, unresolved issues and conflicts. They must be cognizant of client-elicited emotions, counter-transference and other issues that impact counseling relationships and must obtain appropriate assistance to deal with such in their personal lives. At the same time, clinical mental health counselors must not accept clients who are not compatible and who might induce or enhance unhealthy personal feelings.

If, after accepting a client, clinical mental health counselors find the counseling relationship is or may be impaired for any reason, they must terminate the counseling relation, transfer the client to another mental health professional, obtain appropriate supervision and include, as necessary, a co-counselor. Clients must be involved in the process and fully informed as to the purpose of any change in treatment.

Clinical mental health counselors who are impaired for any reason are encouraged to use necessary and appropriate rehabilitation and recovery mechanisms. They must be given the full support of the profession during the rehabilitation and recovery process.

Clinical mental health counselors who are impaired and who successfully complete appropriate rehabilitation and recovery program will be expected to develop and maintain a comprehensive supervision plan equaling the ratio of one (1) hour supervision for every fifteen (15) hours of direct client services for a minimum period of not less than three (3) years, and longer if deemed necessary by the counselor, supervisor, or any other authority.

Association of Visual Language Interpreters of Canada

<u>CODE OF ETHICS</u>

1. The visual language interpreter will keep all assignment-related information strictly confidential.

2. The visual language interpreter will render the message by faithfully conveying its intent and spirit.

3. The visual language interpreter will not counsel, advise or interject personal opinions related to the interpreted assignment.

4. The visual language interpreter will use the preferred language of the person(s) for whom she/he is interpreting.

5. The visual language interpreter will accept assignments using discretion with regard to the interpreting skills required, the setting, and the person(s) involved.

6. The visual language interpreter will approach the matter of compensation in a fair and equitable manner.

7. The visual language interpreter will conduct herself/himself in all phases of the interpreting situation in a manner befitting the profession.

8. The visual language interpreter will strive to further individual knowledge and skill in order to maintain high professional standards.

Adopted 1983

Registry of Interpreters For The Deaf

CODE OF ETHICS

1. Interpreter/transliterator shall keep all assignment-related information strictly confidential.

2. Interpreter/transliterator shall render the message faithfully, always conveying the content and spirit of the speaker, using language most readily understood by the person(s) whom they serve.

3. Interpreter/transliterator shall not counsel, advise or interject personal opinions.

4. Interpreter/transliterator shall accept assignments using discretion with regard to skill, setting, and the consumers involved.

5. Interpreter/transliterator shall request compensation for services in a professional and judicious manner.

6. Interpreter/transliterator shall function in a manner appropriate to the situation.

7. Interpreter/transliterator shall strive to further knowledge and skills through participation in workshops, professional meetings, interaction with professional colleagues and reading of current literature in the field.

8. Interpreter/transliterator, by virtue of membership in or certification by RID, Inc. shall strive to maintain high professional standards in compliance with the Code of Ethics.

As revised, 1979.

References and Reading List

American Heritage Dictionary, Third Edition. 1992.

Baker, N. Larry. 1996. Becoming the Kind of Person Who
... The Church and the Formation of Character in
Christian Ethics Today, Vol. 2, No. 4, November.

Biggs, Donald & Blocher, Donald. 1987. *Foundations
ofEethical Counseling.* New York, NY: Springer
Publishing Company.

Broadus, Loren. 1996. *Ethics for REAL People.* St. Louis,
Mo.: Chalice Press.

Canadian Psychological Association. 1986. A Canadian
Code of Ethics for Psychologists. Ottawa: Canadian
Psychological Association.

Corey, Gerald, Marianne Corey, and Patrick Callanan.
1993. *Issues and Ethics in the Helping Professions.*
Pacific Grove, CA: Brooks/Cole Publishing Company.

DeGBono, Edward. 1998. *Thinking for Action.* New York,
NY: DK Publishing.

"Does Character Count?" *U.S. News and World Report*,
June 24, 1996, 35.

Ehrenhart, Alan. 1996. Character Making American
Comeback in *The American Daily Town Talk,* July 10.

"Ethical Principles For College And University Teaching:
Canadian Professors Define Their Professional
Responsibilities As Teachers" 1996. *Society for
Teaching and Learning in Higher Education.*

Fant, Lou. 1990. *Silver Threads.* Silver Spring, Md.: RID
Publications.

Frankl, V. 1959. *Man's Search For Meaning.* New York:
Washington Square Press.

Fretz, B. R. and Mills, D. H. 1980. *Licensing and Certification of Psychologists and Counselors.* San Francisco: Jossey-Bass.

God's Little Instruction Book Series, Vol. I, II, III. 1997. Tulsa, OK: Honor Books, Inc.

Gough, Russell W. 1998. *Character Is Destiny: The Value Of Personal Ethics In Everyday Life.* Rocklin, Ca: Prima Publishing.

Hanson, Wes and Michael. Josephson (Ed). 1998 *The Power of Character.* San Francisco, CA: Jossey-Bass

Herlihb, B. and Golden L. B. 1990. *AACD Ethical Standards Casebook* (4th Ed). Alexandria, VA: American Association for Counseling and Development.

Humphrey, Janice H. and Alcorn, Bob J. 1996. *So You Want To Be An Interpreter?* Amarillo, TX: H & H Publishers.

Kain, C. D. 1988. To Breach or Not to Breach: Is That the Question? A response to Gary and Harding. *Journal of Counseling and Development.* 66(5), 224-225.

Lane, Harlan. 1984. *When The Mind Hears: A History Of The Deaf.* New York: Random House.

Levinson, J. L. 1986. When a Colleague Practices Unethically: Guidelines for Intervention. *Journal of Counseling and DevelopmentI.* 64(5), 315-317.

Levy, Charles S., DSW. 1993. *Social Work Ethics On The Line.* New York, NY: Haworth Press.

McCuen. 1990. Leadership and Professional Ethics. In *Reflections on Ethics: A Compilation of Articles Inspired by the May 1990 ASHA Ethics Colloquium.* Silver Sprint, Md: American Speech and Hearing Association.

Microsoft® Encarta® 98 Encyclopedia. *The American Heritage® Concise Dictionary*, 3ʳᵈ Edition. 1994. New York: Houghton Mifflin Co. Electronic version licensed from and portions copyright © 1994 by INSO Corporation.

Muehleman, T., Pickens, Bl and Robinson, F. 1985. Informing Clients about the Limits to Confidentiality, Risks and Their Rights: Is Self-Disclosure Inhibited? *Professional Pyschology: Research and Practice*. 16(34), 385-397.

Neufeldt, Victoria. 1996. *Webster's New World College Dictionary*, 3ʳᵈ Edition. New York: MacMillan Press.

Pettifor, Jean L. 1991. How Well Does The Canadian Code Of Ethics Serve Community Psychologists? *Psynopsis*, Winter, 1-12.

Rest, J. 1979. *Development In Judging Moral Issues*. Minneapolis, MN: University of Minnesota Press.

Rest, J. 1984. Research On Moral Development: Implications For Training Psychologists. *The Counseling Psychologist*, 12, 19-30.

Schulz, William E. 1994. *Counselling Ethics Casebook*. Ottawa, ON: Canadian Guidance and Counselling Association.

Schlessinger, Laura. 1996. *How Coule You Do That?! The Abdication of Character, Courage and Conscience*. New York, NY: Harper Collins

Seeley, J. 1964. Social Work: Possibilities, Purposes And Powers in *The Social Worker*, Nov. 7-19.

Seymour, C. 1990. The Hunt For Absolute Goodness. In *Reflections On Ethics: A Compilation Of Articles Inspired by the May 1990 ASHA Ethics Colloquium*. Silver Spring, MD: American Speech and Hearing Association.

Sheeley, V. L. & Herlihy, B. 1986. The Ethics of Confidentiality and Priviledged Communication. *Journal of Counseling and Human Service Professions*. 1(1), 141-148.

Sociological Practice Association. 1987. *Ethical Standards of Sociological Practitioners* (rev. ed). Chester, NY: Author.

Stadler, Holly A. 1986b. To Counsel or Not to Counsel: The Ethical Dilemma of Dual Relationships. *Journal of Counseling and Human Service Professions*, 1(1), 134-140.

Stadler, Holly A. 1985. *Confidentiality: The Professionals' Dilemma*. AACD Video Cassette Series. Alexandria, Va.: American Association for Counseling and Development Foundation.

Stromberg, D. 1990. Key Legal Issues In Professional Ethics. In Reflections on *Ethics: A Compilation Of Articles Inspired By The May 1990 ASHA Ethics Colloquium*. Silver Spring, MD: American Speech and Hearing Association.

Woody, R. 1984. Professional Responsibilities and Liabilities. In R. Woody (Ed.) *The Law and the Practice of Human Services*. San Francisco: Jossey-Bass.

Index

A

Accountability 65, 68, 69, 74, 84, 124
Aintablian v
American Sign Language Teachers Association (ASLTA)
.... v, 50, 51
Applying the Standards
  Aardvark 96
  Arabesque 59
  Armadillo 117
  Armoire 58
  Beammer 126
  Beammette 48
  Blubyrd 100
  Charlemagne 54
  Cocktail 116
  Daffodil 86
  Diction 89
  Douglas College 120
  Dragonfly 55
  Dynomite 61
  Egret 129
  Emmylou 66
  Fansie Fingers 122
  Fantasie 46
  Jackpot 135
  KarmelKorn 125
  Lobelia 103
  Neopreme 76
  Nutmeg 119
  Oak 79
  OliveOyle 87
  Pepin 101
  Peppermint 106
  Peter Pan 110
  Phroofroo 74
  Phrootloop 111
  Popeye 72

Quark 97
Rhino... 73
Skateboard 132
Thyme 81
Vanna Bannanna 136
Whiz 131
Zebra...138
Zenith...70, 115
Appropriate Community Interaction 44
Arnell v
ASL Teachers
  Boundaries... 93
  Certification.. 50
  Community endorsement... 49
  Community interactions... 98
  Confidentiality 113
  Continuing education.. 60
  Cultural norms.. 43
  Educational requirements 49
  Fair and unbiased 108
  Participation in professional associations 62
  Professional associations 50
  Professional development 39
  Professional relationships 91
  Qualifications..47, 49
  Quality of Service... 80
  Sharing student informaton 114
Association of Visual Language Interpreters of Canada
  (AVLIC) ....v, 51, 52, 68
Audism..108

B

Baker..2, 3, 29
Bice v
Bilingual and Bicultural Knowledge and Skills
  Definition of 40
Block v
Boundaries
  Physical 94
Boundaries ....
  ....44, 56, 92, 93, 94, 95, 96, 97, 98, 103, 105, 106
  Gifts 99

Physical 93
Psychological 56, 92, 102
Sexual 103
Social Interactions 98
Bridges v
Broadus 1
Burns 80
Burtnik v

C

Canadian Psychological Association .... iv, 18
Carver .... v, 42
Case Studies 145-224
Interpreters 145
Teachers 203
Certification 68
Chan 42
Character
Definition of 3
Clinton 127
Codes of Ethics
American Mental Health Counselors Association 239
American Sign Language Teachers Association (ASLTA)
.... 230
Association of Visual Language Interpreters of Canada
(AVLIC) 253
Canadian Psychological Association 18
Purpose of 5, 6, 9
Psychiatric Nurses Association of Canada 225
Registry of INterpreters for the Deaf (RID) 254
Samples of ....
The Society of Translators and Interpreters of British
Columbia (STIBC) 228

Collegial Support 64, 65
Community endorsement 41
Definition of 42
Community Interactions
Interpreters and Teachers 58
Competent ASL Teacher
Definition of 38, 39
Competent practitioner 37

Competent Sign Language Interpreter
    Definition of 37, 38
Competent Teacher of ASL/English Interpretation
    Definition of 38, 39
Conference of Interpreter Training................................. 51
Confidentiality 8, 9, 10, 23, 32, 34, 35, 71, 75, 102,
    112, 113, 114, 116, 120, 134
    Deaf culture norms of 120
    Limits of 117
    Professional Consultation.. 113
    Sharing pertinent history... 113
Constructive feedback 65
Critical thinking 22, 26, 30, 63
Cultural Norms 43, 57
Culturally appropriate.. 42, 49
Culture
    View of professionalism 56
    aspects of
        cognitive.. 41
        normative 41
        tangible 41

D

Deaf Interpreter
    Definition of 130
Decision-Making Models
    An integrated model 28
    Canadian Psychological Association 20, 27
    Humphrey and Alcorn 26, 27
    Overview.. 27
    Stadler 22, 27
Decision-Making Process
    Example of 32
Derosiers.. v
Douglas College iv
Duty to Report.. 112
    Clients must be informed.. 116

E

Empowerment 107, 109
Ethical dilemma
    Example of 13, 14

Ethical integrity...111
Ethical Vigilance...63, 64
Ethics
    Definition of 2
    Dictionary definition 1
    Right conduct 7

F

Fant...5
Feedback 60, 64, 123, 124, 127
Fees for Professional Services 85
    Cultural norms..87
    sliding scale...85
Ferguson v
Frankl...6, 29
Free from Bias 74

G

Giroux v
Guidelines 139

H

Harassment 108
Hall..v
Hold clients needs primary 85
Howard...v
Humphrey & Alcorn 6, 8, 24, 39
Humphries...108

I

Informed Consent...114
Interests of Clients Held Primary.........................105
Interpreter qualifications................................45
Interpreters
    Boundaries...93
    Certification requirements 52
    Community interaction 58
    Confidentiality 113
    Continuing education...............................60
    Educational requirements 52
    Fair and unbiased 108

Language abilities...45
Participation in professional associations.....................62
Personal accountability 53
Professional relationships 91
Qualifications...49, 53
Quality of Service 80
Working relationships 112

J

Jenkins .... v, 42
Jickels... v, 42

K

Kemp... v, 42
Kerry 127

L

Lane 57
Lawrence v
Legality
    Definition of 2
Legislated Behavior..9
Levy..6, 7

M

Magirescu.. v, 42
Making Ethical Decisions...6, 7
Malcolm... v
Manipulation of Work Situation 105
McCuen 7
McLaughlin.. v, 42
Marbury... v
Meta-Ethical Principles 10, 17, 20, 21, 22, 24, 28, 33
    Autonomy..13
    Autonomy and Self Determination.............................25
    Autonomy/empowerment 11, 14, 21
    Canadian Psychological Association 18
    Communication access 25
    Definition 10
    Do Good 11, 12, 13, 21
    Do no harm 11, 13, 14, 21
    Equality 21

Examples of..11, 12, 13, 14
Informed Consent...11, 25
Integrity in relationships 11, 13, 18
Justice and equality...11, 12
Keeping promises...29, 33
Not willfully harming others................................29, 33
Personal dignity and equality 25
Privacy/confidentiality..25
Protection of the weak and vulnerable..........................11
Respect for the dignity of persons.............................18
Respecting the right for self-determination 29
Responsibility to society 18, 29, 33
Responsible Caring 11, 13, 18, 29, 33
Right to self-determination 33
Sanctity of life...29
Self-Determination/Empowerment....................107, 109
Self evolution...25
Shultz...29
Sign Language Model..24
Stadler..21
Models for Ethical Decision-Making................................17
Moral Conduct...9
Morality
    Definition of 2
Morés 3

P

Palmer.. v
Personal Appearance 77
Personal Bias 109
Personal Gain...105, 107
Personal Responsibility 65, 84
Philip..41, 44
Preparing for Work..80
Professional
    Cultural definitions 56
    Deaf view...57
    Definition of 56
Professional Associations..62
Professional Competence..37
Professional Consultation 95, 133
Professional Criteria..83

Professional Development..60
Professional Distance..56
Professional Image..77, 81
Professional qualifications
    Claiming credentials 68
Professional Relationships 91
Professional Standards..9
Professional work ethic..15
Professionals
    definition of...5
    Trustworthy 7
Protocol..8, 38, 39, 128

Q

Qualifications 71
    Misrepresentation of..69
Quality of Service..124
Quotation Box .... vi, 4, 24, 30, 78

R

Record Keeping 137
Registry of Interpreters for the Deaf................ v, 51, 52, 68
Roy.. v
Russell.. v

S

Safe Learning Environment
    Definition of 121, 123
Schulz .... iv, 28, 30, 31, 32, 33
Self-Determination..109
Sexual Abuse..112
Seymour..49
Sign Language Instructors of Canada (SLIC).....................50
Sign Language Interpreter
    Education required..38
Social Interactions..98
Stadler..18, 21, 22, 23
Stereotyping 108
Stromberg 9
Subpoenaed to Testify 116, 117
Systems..39, 132, 134

T

Teacher of ASL/English Interpretation
  Education...38
  Professional development 39
Teachers
  Community interaction 58
Teachers of ASL
  Cultural norms...42
Teachers of ASL/English Interpretation
  Boundaries...93
  Certification requirements 51
  Community endorsement...51
  Confidentiality 113
  Continuing education..60
  Cultural norms..43
  Educational requirements 51
  Fair and unbiased 108
  Participation in professional associations 62
  Professional relationships 91
  Qualifications...47, 49
  Quality of Service 80
  Sharing student information 114
Terminology 1
Timeliness 84

U

Unable to do the Task
  Self-removal...128

V

Values 3, 35
Vulnerable Individuals..112

W

Webster 2, 8
Work Ethic 63